Praise For

THE UNOFFENDABLE WIFE

It is a rare and powerful thing to encounter a devotional that not only speaks truth, but lives it. *The Unoffendable Wife* is exactly that a life transforming journey rooted in daily Scripture, thoughtful reflection, and practical, actionable steps that have the power to truly shift the course of a marriage.

What makes this book even more impactful is the integrity behind it. When you know the lives of the author, the words carry a deeper weight. Misty's journey (even in writing this book) is one that ONLY came from obedience to God. She and her husband Matt don't just write about a godly, thriving marriage - they exemplify it. Their lives reflect conviction, humility, and a genuine pursuit of the Lord that is both inspiring and inviting.

In a world where the truth about marriage has too often been distorted, her devotional stands as a refreshing and ridiculously amazing guide back to God's design. One that is full, purposeful, and anchored in Him.

No matter what season of marriage you find yourself in, this book meets you there. It gently calls you closer to the heart of the Father, reminding us that as we draw near to Him,He faithfully draws near to us.

It is truly an honor to know Matt and Misty, to learn from them, and to run alongside them. We wholeheartedly encourage you not to just read this book. *Live it.* Let it shape your heart, your perspective, and your marriage.

It is, without a doubt, an incredible gift. Seriously though, read it and do the thangs and it will without a doubt impact your life!

With Our Full Celebration and Support,
Micah & Sara Zell
Founders & Senior Leaders of Christ Culture International

After the first few chapters, I quickly realized this was a book I didn't even know I needed. It gently challenged me to reflect on something I hadn't really considered before: *Do I get offended by my husband?*

What makes this book so powerful is that it's not only insightful, but also incredibly practical. The message is clear, relatable, and easy to follow, with a call to action that feels both specific and attainable. At the same time, it leaves just enough space for the Lord to step in—bringing conviction, encouragement, and a deeper awareness of our hearts.

It was such a blessing to finally have words for some of these difficult but important topics. Misty, thank you for being obedient and bold enough to share your stories and remind us of these biblical truths. Because of this book, we can all grow to be better spouses and in turn deepen our relationship with Christ.

Let this book be an invitation for you to have more connection, awareness, and prayer in your marriage. This book feels like a gift—to me, to my marriage, and to the friends and family I'll be sharing it with. And for the record... my husband thanks you too!

Michelle K.

In The Unoffendable Wife, Misty Parenzan offers a deeply insightful and Spirit-led devotional for women who desire peace and wholeness in their marriage. With honesty and grace, she guides readers through real-life moments of offense, revealing how a surrendered heart can become a dwelling place for God's peace.

This 30-day journey is more than a devotional—it is an invitation to inner transformation. Misty gently reminds us that as we yield our hearts to the Lord, He brings healing, restores joy, and strengthens the covenant of marriage. A timely and hope-filled resource for any woman longing to cultivate a softer heart and a stronger, Christ-centered relationship.

Jane Hamon
Bishop at Vision Church @ Christian International

You hold in your hands a timely and much-needed tool for today—one that can transform you, your marriage, and your family. In fact, its reach extends even further, with the potential to strengthen any relationship as you follow the devotional Misty has so beautifully laid out.

In a world that encourages us to fight for our rights and our way, Misty offers a biblical, Kingdom-minded approach to relationships. This is a call to see others through God's eyes rather than our emotions—and to watch what He does in our relationships.

Lynn Copeland
Author & Speaker; Co-Author of Breakthrough Prayers for Moms, A Prayers That Avail Much Resource

the unoffendable wife

the unoffendable wife

30 days to a *softer* heart
& stronger marriage

Misty Parenzan

NINE ARROWS
media

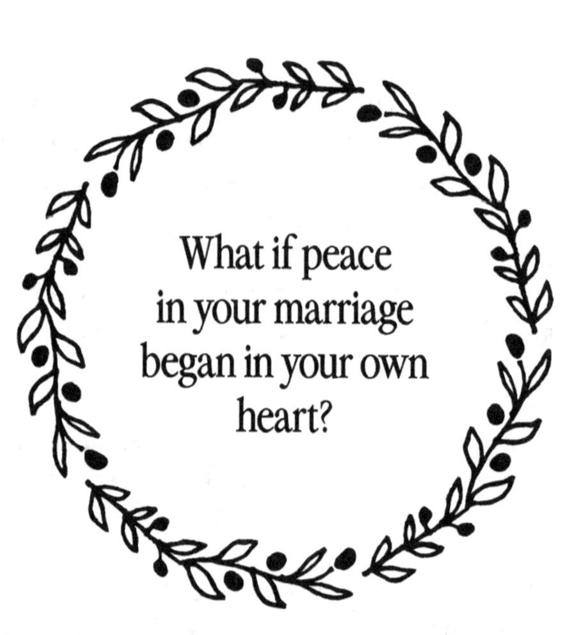
What if peace
in your marriage
began in your own
heart?

*For my
husband, Matt*

My living reminder that grace always wins.

Through you, God has taught me what it
means to love like Jesus—and to let His peace
guard my heart.

TABLE of CONTENTS

Foreword
BY MATT PARENZAN

Marriage has a way of revealing things about us we didn't know were there. Not the big, obvious things—but the small ones.
The quick reactions.
The tone in our voice.
The assumptions we carry.
The subtle ways pride shows up in ordinary moments.

After more than twenty years of marriage and raising nine children together, Misty and I have learned something: Most of the tension in marriage doesn't come from the big moments. It comes from the small ones—the everyday interactions where offense quietly tries to take root.

A comment taken the wrong way.
A tone that lands harder than intended.
A moment where pride wants to respond faster than love.

And what we consistently think about—whether good or bad, in our marriage or within ourselves—shapes what we look for and ultimately what we see.

A few years ago, Misty felt the Lord invite her into something that seemed simple on the surface, but carried a deep and weighty work within her heart. And for thirty days, she would choose not to let offense take root toward me.

She embraced the posture and principle: *Guard the gate of your heart—it determines what your mind will dwell on.*

She didn't announce it.
She didn't make a big deal about it.
She just quietly began living it out—what she calls *"the pause before the pounce."*

And what happened next surprised both of us. Our conversations softened. The atmosphere in our home shifted. Moments that once would have escalated... simply didn't. Not because everything was perfect. But because my wife *chose* to guard her heart.

Scripture says, "Good sense makes one slow to anger, and it is his glory to overlook an offense."

Overlooking offense isn't weakness. It's strength under control. It's choosing humility when pride wants to rise. Patience when reaction feels justified. Grace when frustration would be easier. Because peace is either received as a gift... or surrendered by what we allow.

One day Misty shared with me what she had been doing.

"God challenged me not to let you offend me."

I remember laughing at first. But the more I thought about it, the more I realized—something powerful had taken place. My wife made a decision that protected her heart, our marriage, and the atmosphere of our home.

This book is the fruit of that journey.

What you're about to read is not about ignoring problems, pretending everything is fine, or suppressing real emotions. Misty makes that clear.

This is about positioning your heart before God—the place where reactions are formed, where thoughts take shape, and where peace is either cultivated or compromised.

An unoffendable heart isn't passive.
It's powerful. It takes strength to pause when your instinct is to react. It takes humility to choose reconciliation over being right. It takes courage to let love lead instead of pride.

But when someone chooses that path, something remarkable happens: *Peace begins to grow where tension once lived.*

To the wives reading this:
Your willingness to pursue this kind of heart posture matters more than you know. It has the power to change you. To shift

the atmosphere of your home. To soften conversations. To create space for God to work in ways you may not immediately see. And to your surprise—it may very well be the spark, the catalyst, that opens your husband's eyes to see, his ears to hear, and his heart to become the man God has called him to be.

To the husbands whose wives choose this path:
Don't take that grace lightly.
Honor it.
Respond to it.
Steward it well.
Reciprocate it.
"Be devoted to one another in love. Honor one another above yourselves"

Marriage was never designed to be a scoreboard. It was designed to be a covenant. A place where forgiveness replaces resentment. Where humility disarms pride. Where peace becomes stronger than offense.

Misty wrote this book with honesty, wisdom, and a deep love for women who desire peace in their marriages. She knows the struggle. She knows the pull to react. And she knows the freedom that comes when offense no longer gets the final say.

My prayer is that as you walk through this journey, you discover what many of us learn over time: Peace in a marriage rarely begins by changing the other person. More often, it begins when

God changes our heart. And when one heart chooses grace, it has the power to transform an entire home. A strong marriage isn't formed by controlling outcomes, but by becoming people anchored in truth.

When we live from who we are in Christ, peace stops being a hope—and becomes the atmosphere of our home.

Matt Parenzan

AN INVITATION TO THE JOURNEY

Sweet friend,

If you're holding this book, I believe it's because something inside you is stirring.

Maybe it's a quiet longing for peace and connection, a desire to love more freely and to soften the tension that's been building between you and the man you love.

Maybe you've been walking on eggshells, weary from the little things that add up.

Or maybe you just sense there's more... more joy, more grace, more love waiting on the other side of offense.

I've been there too.
I know what it's like to take things personally, to replay the same frustrations, to want change but not know where to start.

What began as a simple challenge between me and God, thirty days of not letting my husband offend me, became a heart reset that changed everything.

But this isn't just another book.
It's a sacred invitation.

An invitation to slow down, to soften, and to let God meet you in the small spaces between frustration and peace... between pride and surrender... between reacting and responding.

You don't need a perfect marriage or a spotless heart, just a willing one. Over these next thirty days, you'll learn to pause before reacting, to pray before speaking, and to let the Holy Spirit transform you from the inside out.

This journey isn't about *striving*. It's about *surrender*.
It's not about fixing your husband. It's about allowing God to refine you.

As you walk through each day, you'll begin to notice something beautiful: peace will rise where tension once lived, gratitude will replace irritation, and love will become your loudest response.

So take a deep breath and open your heart wide. Let this be your yes to healing, to growth, to a love that no longer bends under offense.

God's not asking for perfection; He's inviting you into partnership... one pause, one prayer, one act of grace at a time.

Welcome to

The Unoffendable Wife.
Your 30-day marriage reset
begins now.

With love and expectation,

Misty Parenzan

Before you begin, please read this prayerfully.

This journey is meant to bring freedom, peace, and healing - but it also needs to be walked with wisdom, safety, and grace.

This 30-day challenge was written for wives in safe, loving marriages who desire deeper connection, peace, and spiritual growth. It's about softening, not staying silent; pausing, not pretending.

If your relationship involves abuse, manipulation, addiction, or emotional or spiritual control, this devotional is not meant for that season. Choosing grace does not mean tolerating mistreatment. God's heart is for your healing, safety, and peace.

Please reach out to a trusted counselor, pastor, or friend if you are in an unsafe or unstable situation. You are deeply loved, fully seen, and worthy of a life marked by freedom and wholeness.

God never asks you to remain where harm or fear rule. His love always makes a way toward safety and restoration.

With that foundation in place, let's step into this together...
open-hearted, anchored in truth, and covered in grace.

The Heart Behind
THE UNOFFENDABLE WIFE

Marriage has a way of revealing what's really inside us - not to shame us, but to shape us.

The little irritations, the misunderstandings, the tone that hits wrong, the unmet expectations... they all become mirrors, reflecting what's still being refined within us.

For years, I believed peace in marriage meant my husband needed to change. But the truth I discovered was deeper: peace began when I did.

If you've read my first book, *He Was Always There*, you already know a piece of our story...how God met me in the middle of brokenness, healed deep wounds, and redeemed what once felt beyond repair. That book tells how faith restored my life; this one shows how that same faith continues to deepen my marriage.

The Unoffendable Wife was born out of the lessons that came after the miracle, the daily choices, the quiet surrenders, the refining work that turned revelation into a new rhythm.

It started with a challenge I felt came from the Lord. Thirty days of choosing not to let offense take root. Thirty days of catching my reactions, softening my words, choosing joy, and letting the Holy Spirit interrupt my impulses.

What happened in those thirty days changed everything. The atmosphere in our home shifted. My tone softened. My joy returned. And for the first time in a long time, I felt truly free.

Not because Matt became perfect, but because my heart became protected by peace.

That's what this book is about: learning to pause before reacting and pray before speaking...loving in ways that disarm offense before it even has a chance to grow.

The Unoffendable Wife is a journey of transformation. One that starts in the heart and spills out into every part of your home.

Over the next 30 days, you'll learn to:
• Guard your heart without hardening it
• Speak life even when it's hard
• Choose peace over being right
• Forgive in real time
• Love without a hook

It's not about perfection. It's about presence.

It's choosing to show up in your marriage with patience, humility, meekness, and grace that comes from God alone.

If you let Him, He will use this challenge to rewrite your reactions, heal old hurts, and fill your home with the kind of love that endures.

You don't have to strive. You just have to surrender.

You're about to discover the beauty of becoming an unoffendable wife.

PROLOGUE

The Challenge That Changed Everything

It was January 2021, shortly after completing what has now become one of my favorite marriage teachings, Paul David Tripp's *What Did You Expect*.

I'd just finished watching the video series with a few other couples, and something about his message stirred deep within.

I decided to try a personal experiment. For the next thirty days, I made a promise to myself and to God that I would not let my husband offend me.

No matter what he did, whether he came home later than he said, dropped his boxers next to the hamper instead of in it, spent hours piddling in the garage, played on his phone too long, or used my toothpaste and left it on the counter, I was determined not to let those little things get under my skin.

I didn't tell Matt. I didn't mark it on the calendar or announce it like some grand challenge. It was simply a quiet whisper from the Lord: *Lay down your reactions and let Me teach you peace in real time.*

At that point in our marriage, things were good but not always peaceful. That January we would celebrate eighteen years together, and our youngest was four, so we were finally past the baby years. With only five of our nine kids left at home, life had settled into a steady rhythm, but even in that calm, something felt off. It wasn't the big arguments that wore us down. It was all the small stuff: the sideways comments, the tone that rubbed wrong, the interruptions that hit at the worst possible time.

And I'll be honest... I could pounce fast. A sigh, a sarcastic comment, a look that said really? before I even realized it. But I began to notice how much those quick reactions cost us. They chipped away at closeness and built invisible walls that kept us from truly connecting.

So that January, I decided to try something different.
What if, for thirty days, I refused to take offense?
What if I paused instead of pounced?
What if I asked God to help me see Matt through His eyes instead of through my emotions?

The first few days were humbling. I didn't realize how many times a day I had the opportunity to be offended. I'd feel irritation rise, and in that moment, I'd hear the Holy Spirit whisper, *"Pause before you pounce."*

So, I did. I paused and prayed and prayed some more. And slowly, peace began to take root.

When Matt walked in late from work and I greeted him with a smile instead of a cold shoulder, he noticed. When I didn't huff about the laundry or the toothpaste, he noticed even more. My willingness to let go of offense was creating a whole new atmosphere in our home and in me, one marked by gentleness instead of tension.

By the end of the month, the change was undeniable. Our intimacy deepened. Our communication softened. Those small annoyances that once stole my peace no longer had the same power.

At the beginning of the next month, Matt left town on a trip. In the past those trips had always been a sore spot. Anytime he went away—whether for work, golf, or anything extra—I'd find a reason to be upset. I'd grow distant, give him the cold shoulder, be snappy, and make sure he knew I wasn't happy about it.

But this time was different.

Because I had just come off that 30-day challenge, I didn't want to lose the peace we'd found. When he called, I answered with warmth and told him how much I loved and missed him, and how proud I was of him. I even made sure the kids got to talk to him each day.

When he came home, I'll never forget the look on his face. He studied me for a moment and said, "What's going on with you? You're… different. Are you okay?"

I smiled, because he was right. I was different, and it felt so good to finally tell him.

I said, "God challenged me back in January not to let you offend me. I decided to choose peace instead of pride, prayer instead of reaction."

He smiled, shook his head, and said, "That actually makes me feel better. I was beginning to worry."

That one decision transformed our marriage into something I'd never experienced on this side of heaven. Matt hadn't suddenly become a different man, but I had become a different wife. My heart was softer. My tone was gentler. My joy was deeper.

That simple challenge changed more than our communication. It changed me.

It taught me that most of my frustration had less to do with Matt and more to do with my need to control, to be right, to have things my way, my preferences.

Being an unoffendable wife didn't mean I stopped caring. No, it meant I started loving differently. It wasn't about being passive;

it was about being present. It was about creating space for grace instead of feeding frustration.

That's what The Unoffendable Wife was born from... one quiet decision that turned into a lifestyle of peace.

You don't have to have it all together. You just have to start with one decision, to let God meet you in the pause before the pounce.

Here's to one day, one choice, one transformed marriage at a time... and to the quiet miracle that happens when we decide... **offense ends with me.**

How To
USE THIS BOOK

This 30-day challenge isn't about perfection. It's about practice. Each day invites you to pause, reflect, and respond with grace in the moments that test your heart most.

The journey is divided into four phases, each one building on the last, guiding you from awareness to renewal, and finally, to lasting strength. Let the rhythm of these phases slow you down, shape you, and prepare your heart for the transformation God has waiting.

Here's how to walk through it:

1. Read One Day at a Time

Each day includes a Scripture, a short story from my own journey, a reflection, a prayer, a challenge, a decree, and journal prompts. Read slowly. Let the message sink in. Don't rush the process. Growth takes root in the stillness.

2. Reflect & Journal

Use the *Reflection Journal* questions to explore your thoughts,

emotions, and experiences. There's no right answer...
only honesty.

Write your responses, your prayers, your progress, and even
your setbacks. This is your sacred space.

3. Pray the Daily Prayer & Decree Aloud

There's power in speaking God's truth over your heart and
home. The daily prayers will help you surrender control, release
offense, and welcome His peace into every moment.

The decree is your faith in action, aligning your words with
God's promises and inviting His power to bring them to pass.

4. Live the Challenge, Phase by Phase

Each phase represents a part of the journey:
Awareness & Reflection, Softening & Surrender, Connection &
Renewal, and Strength & Legacy. Move through them slowly
and intentionally.

The daily challenges are small acts of obedience that build a new
rhythm of grace, one choice at a time.

5. Extend Yourself Grace

You won't do this perfectly and that's okay.

If you miss a day, start again.

If you stumble, forgive yourself quickly.

Remember, this journey isn't about being *an unoffendable wife* for thirty days; it's about becoming a woman whose heart is learning how to stay free, no matter what.

Take a deep breath, open your heart, and begin.

You're about to discover what happens when love leads, peace protects, and grace becomes your default.

And while this journey is powerful on its own, it was also designed to be lived out together - in community, with grace, and with support.

Using the Unoffendable Wife
AS A 6-WEEK GROUP STUDY

The Unoffendable Wife was written to be experienced personally, but it was also designed to be lived out in community.

While the heart of this journey is daily, personal reflection, walking it alongside other women creates space for deeper healing, encouragement, and grace-filled accountability. When women gather around truth with open hearts, shame loosens its grip, peace multiplies, and transformation takes root.

This 6-week group study allows you to move through the full 30-day journey at a sustainable, unhurried pace, honoring both safety and growth. The first week prepares the heart. The final week helps anchor what God has done.

This is not a study about fixing your husband.
It's about allowing God to refine you, one pause, one prayer, one choice at a time.

The goal is not perfection. It's formation.

THE 6-WEEK STUDY RHYTHM

Week 1 - Orientation & Foundation

Read:

• Letter to the Reader

• A Gentle Note on Safety and Grace

• Introduction

• Prologue

• How to Use This Book

• Group Agreement

Focus: Creating safety, setting expectations, grounding the group in grace

This week is about preparing the soil—establishing trust, normalizing imperfection, and reminding everyone that this is a Spirit-led journey, not a performance.

Week 2 - Awareness & Reflection

Read: Days 1–7

Focus: Pausing before reacting, noticing tone, assumptions, and inner patterns

Week 3 - Softening & Surrender

Read: Days 8–15

Focus: Releasing expectations, forgiving quickly, renewing the mind, letting love lead

Week 4 - Connection & Renewal

Read: Days 16–23

Focus: Listening deeply, gratitude, humility, restoring closeness

Week 5 - Strength & Legacy

Read: Days 24–30

Focus: Guarding peace, speaking life, grace on repeat, unoffendable love

Week 6 - Reflection, Integration & Blessing

Read:

- Final Encouragement
- Beyond the 30 Days
- Prayer of Completion
- Epilogue

Focus: Celebrating growth, anchoring new rhythms, and carrying this posture forward

This final week is not about ending, but about **becoming**.

A Gentle Agreement for Our Group

Before beginning, we agree to the following:

• We share from our own hearts, not our husband's failures

• We listen without fixing or correcting

• We honor different seasons and stories

• We prioritize safety, grace, and humility

This is a place for growth, not judgment.

For healing, not comparison. For grace, not perfection.

Weekly Gathering Flow (Simple & Flexible)

Each gathering can follow this gentle rhythm:

1. Welcome & Prayer

2. Scripture Focus for the Week

3. Group Discussion

4. Practice Focus (one small takeaway)

5. Closing Prayer

You don't need to rush. Let grace set the pace.

For Group Leaders

Expanded weekly discussion guides, leader notes, and printable resources are available at <u>mistyparenzan.com</u> to support those facilitating this study.

Whether you're gathering in a living room, a church classroom, or around a kitchen table, my prayer is that this study becomes a safe and sacred space, where hearts soften, peace grows, and love leads.

PHASES

Phase 1: Awareness & Reflection (Days 1–7)
Theme: Seeing what's really happening beneath the surface

This phase helps you notice your own reactions, patterns, and perspectives.

You'll learn to pause, listen, and invite God to show you where peace begins inside your own heart.

Phase 2: Softening & Surrender (Days 8–15)
Theme: Letting go of control and choosing grace

Here, you'll practice releasing old expectations, forgiving faster, and responding instead of reacting.

It's the heart-softening work that allows love to take root again.

Phase 3: Connection & Renewal (Days 16–23)
Theme: Rebuilding closeness and restoring peace

This phase leads you to gratitude, empathy, and healing conversations. You'll begin to notice joy returning and the kind of connection that only grows in humility and grace.

Phase 4: Strength & Legacy (Days 24–30)

Theme: Living unoffendably and protecting what God restored

Here, you'll step into lasting transformation, learning to speak life, guard peace, and model covenant love that leaves a legacy of faith and gentleness.

PHASE 1

Phase 1: Awareness & Reflection (Days 1–7)

Before we can build peace, we have to see what's stealing it.

This first phase invites you to slow down and notice not just your spouse's patterns, but your own.

It's about catching those quick reactions, those tiny irritations, those moments when tone or timing turn small things into big ones.

Here, you'll begin practicing awareness: the sacred pause before reaction, the deep breath before words, the choice to see differently.

This week isn't about fixing him. It's about letting God gently hold a mirror to your heart and showing you what He's ready to heal.

PHASE 1 PRAYER

Lord, open my eyes to what You want me to see… about my heart, my reactions, and the roots beneath them. Help me

notice the moments where pride, fear, or insecurity try to steal
my peace. Give me courage to look inward with
honesty and hope.

Let this be a season of awareness that leads to transformation,
not shame. I surrender my assumptions and invite Your truth
to do a gentle work within me.

Amen

PHASE 1 DECREE

I will be quick to listen and slow to react.
God's truth will reveal what emotion tries to hide.
Awareness will lead me to peace, not pride.

PAUSE BEFORE YOU POUNCE

"Everyone should be quick to listen, slow to speak and slow
to become angry."

JAMES 1:19 (NIV)

Early on, I realized that my biggest hurdle in marriage wasn't
the big blowups or major disagreements. It was the tiny, almost
invisible reactions that slipped into the ordinary moments...
those quick, unfiltered responses to the small things.

When Matt would say something offhand that rubbed me the
wrong way, I'd feel that familiar spark rise up inside me.
Without thinking, I'd jump right into a snappy comeback. No
pause, no prayer, no deep breath...just pounce. And that pounce,
more often than not, led to tension that could hang in the air
for hours.

Over time, I began to see a pattern. It wasn't what Matt said that
caused the most damage. It was how I responded. My
defensiveness, my tone, my need to be right. Those tiny

moments were slowly chiseling away at the peace in our home.

But when I started practicing the pause, even just a few seconds to breathe, whisper a quick prayer, or choose silence instead of sarcasm, everything began to shift. That pause gave space for fresh perspective. It allowed the Holy Spirit to speak before my emotions did. It softened my heart and often diffused the tension before it had a chance to grow.

I learned that peace in marriage doesn't come from controlling my spouse's words but from surrendering my own reactions.

REFLECTION

How many arguments could be avoided if we simply paused before we spoke? That pause isn't weakness... it's wisdom. It's the moment we allow God to enter the space between emotion and reaction. When we respond out of love instead of impulse, we protect connection and build trust.

Maybe for you, the "pounce" looks like sarcasm, the silent treatment, or walking away in frustration. Whatever it is, today's challenge is to practice the pause. When something rubs you the wrong way, take a breath, ask God for grace, and choose peace over pride.

CHALLENGE

When irritation rises today, take a deep breath and count to five before responding. Ask the Holy Spirit to fill that pause with wisdom and peace.

At the end of the day, thank God for the moments you paused and invite Him to grow that grace within you.

PRAYER

Lord, teach me to pause before I pounce.
Help me catch my words before they wound and my reactions before they rise.

Fill that space with Your peace.
When I feel misunderstood or irritated, remind me that love listens first and speaks last. Shape my responses so that my marriage reflects Your patience and grace.

Amen

DECREE

I will pause before I pounce.
My words will serve peace, not pride.
The Holy Spirit will lead my reactions and guard my tone.

REFLECTION JOURNAL

Where do you often see offense try to sneak in? How do you plan to handle it differently? What do you notice about your tone body language or thoughts? Do you think pausing will change the outcome?

A pause creates the space where peace can rise
and offense can fade.

CHOOSE CURIOSITY
OVER CRITICISM

"Let your gentleness be evident to all. The Lord is near."

PHILIPPIANS 4:5 (NIV)

Not long after I began my 30-day challenge to stay unoffendable, I had a day that tested me in a whole new way. Matt and I usually connect at least a couple times throughout the day, just quick check-ins to say hi or share a thought, but this particular day, every time I called, I got the same response: "On the other line, call you in 5."

Then later: "In a meeting, can I call you later?" And then… nothing.

By the afternoon, my thoughts started to spiral. He must be avoiding me. If I mattered, he'd make time.

He clearly has time for everyone else today but me.

Each unanswered call stirred up old insecurities, and by the time he finally walked through the door that evening, I was teetering between irritation and full-blown offense.

But then I remembered my challenge.
This was one of those moments...the kind that decides whether peace or pride wins.

So instead of the cold silence or clipped tone that used to come so easily, I took a breath and chose curiosity. I met him at the door, smiled, and asked gently, "Long day?"

He exhaled and said, "You have no idea. Back-to-back calls, missed lunch, nonstop meetings."

In that moment, I saw something I would've completely missed if I'd let offense take over because he wasn't ignoring me:
he was overwhelmed.

That small shift changed everything about the night.
He opened up, I listened, and peace filled the space where tension could have lived.

Curiosity opened a door that criticism would've slammed shut.

REFLECTION

Curiosity says, *"Help me understand."*

Criticism says, *"You're doing it wrong."*
One invites unity; the other breeds division.

When we choose curiosity, we make space for grace. We begin to see that our husbands aren't the enemy...they're human, just like us, with their own unseen pressures, fatigue, and needs.

When we pause long enough to ask a question instead of make a judgment, we discover what's really going on underneath the surface.

Today, when irritation rises, try shifting from accusation to understanding.

Before you assume, *ask.*
Before you react, *wonder.*

This isn't about ignoring real issues. It's about keeping your heart soft enough to hear the truth behind the moment.

CHALLENGE

When your husband says or does something that frustrates you, choose curiosity over criticism.

Instead of assuming or accusing, ask a gentle question like:
• "Are you okay?"
• "Did something happen today?"

• "Can I help with anything?"

Notice how the conversation shifts when you lead with compassion instead of correction.

PRAYER

Lord, help me to see my husband the way You see him. When I'm tempted to criticize, give me the grace to be curious instead. Teach me to ask questions, to listen, and to look beyond what I see.

Guard my heart from assumptions and replace them with understanding. May my words bring life, not judgment, and my tone invite peace, not pride.

Amen

DECREE

I choose curiosity over criticism.
I will look for understanding instead of fault.
Grace will open doors where judgment once closed them.

What moment today tempted you toward criticism? How did curiosity change the outcome? What did you learn about your husband's heart or your own? How can you make curiosity your default response in marriage?

Curiosity opens the door to connection;
criticism closes it.

SEE HIS EFFORT,
NOT HIS ERROR

"Encourage one another and build each other up."

It was a Saturday morning, and Matt had taken it upon himself to "help" by doing some laundry. I walked in just in time to see him doing it all wrong, mixing lights and darks, ignoring fabrics, skipping stain treatment, and filling the machine to the brim.

My first instinct was to correct him. I wanted to say, "That's not how it's done!" But as I opened my mouth, I caught myself because he was helping.

I paused, took a breath, and let it go. He wasn't trying to frustrate me; he was trying to lighten my load.

Later that day, when I walked in and saw him laughing with the kids, it hit me. I'd spent so much energy focusing on how he did things that I'd been missing why he did them. His heart was in the right place, even if his laundry method wasn't.

I realized how many moments I'd robbed us both of joy; times I'd corrected instead of appreciated or critiqued instead of celebrated.

That day, God gently reminded me: connection is built through gratitude, not perfection.

REFLECTION

It's easy to spot what's wrong. Our eyes are trained to notice flaws, fix problems, and improve systems. But in marriage, that mindset can slowly erode gratitude.

When we constantly correct, we unintentionally communicate: *"Your best isn't enough."*

When we choose to notice effort instead, we say: *"I see you trying, and it matters."*

Love covers. It doesn't critique every corner.

Today, let's practice seeing our husband's heart before his habits. When we look for effort, we'll find reasons to be thankful. When we look for errors, we'll find endless reasons to be offended. The lens you choose will determine the atmosphere of your home.

CHALLENGE

Today, look for one specific thing your husband does, even if it's imperfect, and thank him for it. Resist the urge to correct or "fix" the way he does it. Speak life instead of instruction.

Example: "I really appreciate how you handled that," or "Thanks for taking care of that, I noticed."

Watch how gratitude softens the moment and invites closeness.

PRAYER

Lord, open my eyes to see the good in my husband today. Help me to notice his effort, his heart, and the ways he shows love, even if they look different from mine.

Guard my tongue from criticism and fill it with gratitude. Teach me to celebrate progress, not perfection, and to honor him the way You honor me in grace and truth.

Amen

DECREE

I will see my husband's heart before his habits.
Gratitude will be my lens, not correction.
Love will cover what perfection cannot.

REFLECTION JOURNAL

When was the last time I focused on his effort instead of his error? How does my response change the tone of our home? What simple act of appreciation can I express more often? How does gratitude shift my heart toward peace and partnership?

Gratitude sees the heart;
criticism only sees the habit.

4

RELEASE
THE SCORECARD

"Love keeps no record of wrongs."

1 CORINTHIANS 13:5 (NIV)

There was a season in my marriage when I didn't even realize I was keeping score...but I was.

If Matt forgot something I'd mentioned, that was one point.
If he set his alarm too early just to hit snooze, another point.
If he arrived home later than expected, another point.
If I'd picked his boxers up three times in a row, I mentally noted that too.

Over time, those points built a quiet wall between us. It wasn't explosive or obvious...it was subtle and silent. But it made me feel justified when I withdrew or snapped. After all, *I was ahead on the scoreboard.*

One day, while I was mentally tallying a list of what he hadn't done, I felt the Holy Spirit whisper: *"Do you want to win... or do you want to love?"*

That stopped me cold.

Because keeping score might make me feel *right*...but it was robbing me of peace, joy, and connection.

So, I started to intentionally erase the marks. When Matt forgot something, I let it go. When he did something kind, I noticed it instead. Slowly, I realized the only score that mattered was grace, the kind that can't be counted.

REFLECTION

Love doesn't keep records; it keeps perspective.

When we keep score, we shift the focus from we to me. Every offense becomes proof that we're giving more, doing more, trying harder. But love doesn't demand equality.
It offers generosity.

Releasing the scorecard isn't about ignoring pain or pretending things don't hurt. It's about refusing to let small imbalances become big barriers. It's choosing to live in forgiveness rather than fairness. Because let's face it, life isn't fair.

When we stop counting wrongs, we start counting blessings. When we look for errors, we'll find endless reasons to be offended. The lens you choose will determine the atmosphere of your home.

CHALLENGE

Every time you're tempted to mentally "score" something your husband did or didn't do today, stop and whisper, "Grace wins." Instead of keeping a record, keep a prayer list, and thank God for one thing your husband *did right* each time you notice something that frustrates you.

PRAYER

Lord, help me to lay down my invisible scorecard. When I'm tempted to keep track of what he's done, or hasn't done, remind me that love keeps no record of wrongs. Teach me to celebrate progress, not perfection.

Replace resentment with gratitude and comparison with compassion. May my heart be marked by mercy.

Amen

DECREE

I lay down the need to keep score.
Grace wins every time.
My marriage will be marked by mercy.

REFLECTION JOURNAL

What "scores" have I been silently keeping? How has that affected the way I see or speak to my husband? What might change if I started keeping track of his wins instead? How can I remind myself that love's math is always mercy?

Keeping score builds walls;
giving grace builds unity.

CHOOSE RECONCILIATION OVER BEING RIGHT

"Blessed are the peacemakers, for they shall be called
sons of God."

MATTHEW 5:9 (ESV)

There was a night early in our marriage when Matt and I were in the middle of a disagreement. I can't even remember what it was about now...something small that had spiraled into something bigger.

I remember standing in the kitchen, arms crossed, waiting for him to admit that I was right. The silence between us felt heavy, and all I could think was *"If he would just say he's wrong, we could move on."*

Looking back now, I wish I had handled that moment differently.

At the time, I didn't understand how much more valuable

reconciliation was than being right. I hadn't yet learned the power of softening my heart before defending my point.

If I could go back to that night, I would choose peace over pride. I would've taken a deep breath, lowered my tone, and said something simple like, "Let's just start over."

But I wasn't there yet. I was still learning.
And honestly, I think that's where so many of us find ourselves...wanting connection but clinging to control, desiring peace but fighting for victory.

It took years and the Holy Spirit's patient work in me to realize that being "right" rarely brings peace. It may win an argument, but it often loses intimacy.

Since then I've learned that peace is far more satisfying than being right. And reconciliation is always worth more than a momentary win.

REFLECTION

There's something in all of us that wants to prove our point, to be understood, or have the last word. But in marriage, being right can come at the cost of being close.

Reconciliation doesn't mean you ignore truth. It means you value connection enough to pursue peace first. It means humbling yourself, softening your tone, and choosing to restore what offense has broken.

When we let go of our need to win, we make room for God to move. He steps into the gap between our differences and reminds us that peace is His idea, not ours.

Today, ask yourself: *Would I rather be right, or be reconciled?*

CHALLENGE

The next time a disagreement surfaces, pause and ask yourself, *What matters most right now...winning this argument, or protecting our connection?*

Take a deep breath, lower your tone, and if needed, say, "Let's start over." Notice how quickly tension fades when peace becomes the goal instead of proving your point.

PRAYER

Lord, teach me the beauty of reconciliation.
When my pride rises and I want to be right, remind me that
peace matters more.

Give me the courage to lay down my defenses, to soften my
tone, and to choose humility instead of hostility. Help me build
bridges instead of walls.

Let Your Spirit lead me to respond with grace so that unity, not victory, defines my marriage.

Amen

DECREE

I will pursue peace over pride.
Connection matters more than control.
Reconciliation will be the victory I fight for.

REFLECTION JOURNAL

When was the last time you wanted to be "right" more than reconciled? How did that affect your connection with your husband? What does reconciliation look like in your marriage right now? How can you invite the Holy Spirit into your next disagreement?

Winning together matters more
than winning the argument.

6

WHAT YOU FEED GROWS

"Finally, brothers and sisters, whatever is true, whatever is honorable, whatever is just, whatever is pure, whatever is lovely, whatever is commendable, if there is any excellence, if there is anything worthy of praise, think about these things."

PHILIPPIANS 4:8 (NIV)

There was a season when I would wake up and immediately start thinking about all the things Matt did or didn't do. My mind went straight to the little irritations that seemed to multiply overnight.

In the pantry, I'd find half-empty chip bags left open, cracker boxes with just crumbs inside, or snacks tucked away without clips. Instead of tossing them or quietly fixing it, I'd sigh, roll my eyes, and let the frustration simmer.

It wasn't that Matt didn't do good things...it's that I wasn't looking for them. My focus had shifted from gratitude to grievance. Every unclosed bag and unwashed dish became a tiny seed of offense, and I was watering it daily with my thoughts.

One morning, I felt the Holy Spirit nudge me: *What if you stopped counting the crumbs and started counting the blessings?*

That question changed everything.
I grabbed a notebook and started a new kind of list, a "Good Things" list. Each time I noticed something Matt did that blessed our home, no matter how small, I wrote it down. "Made the bed." "Loaded the dishwasher." "Played with the kids." "Sent me a sweet text."

By the end of the week, my heart had shifted.
Not because Matt had suddenly become perfect, but because my perspective had changed.

I was feeding gratitude instead of irritation.
It turns out peace and offense can't grow in the same garden.
What you feed grows.

REFLECTION

Every thought is a seed, and every seed produces fruit.
When we water irritation, frustration, and offense, our hearts grow bitter. But when we nurture gratitude, grace, and love, our

hearts grow soft and strong.

Your marriage will reflect what you choose to magnify.
You can't always control what happens, but you can always
choose what you focus on.

Today, fix your thoughts on what is *good*.
Let praise be your fertilizer and grace be your water.
The more you thank God for your husband, the easier it
becomes to see him the way God does.

CHALLENGE

Start your own "Good Things List" today. Every time you notice
something your husband does, big or small, write it down.

By the end of the day (or week), thank God for the list and speak
one of those things aloud to your husband.

Watch how gratitude changes what you see.

PRAYER

*Lord, help me to guard the garden of my heart. Show me where
I've been feeding frustration instead of faith. Help me plant
words of gratitude and pull up weeds of complaint.*

May my thoughts, my tone, and my focus honor You. Let my

marriage grow in peace because my heart grows in praise.

Amen

DECREE

I will feed gratitude, not grievance.

My thoughts will water peace, not offense.

What I nurture in my heart will flourish in my home.

When was the last time you wanted to be "right" more than reconciled? How did that affect your connection with your husband? What does reconciliation look like in your marriage right now? How can you invite the Holy Spirit into your next disagreement?

*What you focus on will flourish—so choose
what brings peace.*

THE POWER OF
SOFT ANSWERS

"A gentle answer turns away wrath, but a harsh word stirs

up anger."

PROVERBS 15:1 (NIV)

One evening, Matt and I were having what I like to call a "heated discussion." You know the kind where the words are calm, but the tone is anything but. I could feel my frustration bubbling up, and even though I wasn't yelling, my voice carried a sharp edge.

Halfway through my sentence, I saw his expression shift. He wasn't hearing my words anymore, he was reacting to my tone.

That moment stopped me and I realized how often my delivery drowned out my message. I wasn't trying to wound him, but the sting in my voice said otherwise.

I paused, took a breath, and softened my tone. I said the same thing, but with gentleness. And just like that, the atmosphere changed. His shoulders relaxed. His eyes softened. The tension melted away.

It wasn't magic...it was *humility*.
It was the quiet strength of a soft answer.

Over the years, I've learned that softness isn't weakness; it's wisdom wrapped in grace. A soft tone can calm storms that harsh words only make worse.

REFLECTION

Our words carry weight...but our tone carries power. A sharp response may feel justified in the moment, but it often invites more defensiveness, rather than understanding.

Gentleness disarms.
It invites safety instead of shame.
It shows strength under control...what I call meekness, the same kind of strength Jesus displayed when He spoke truth in love.

Being an unoffendable wife doesn't mean staying silent. It means learning to speak with a tone that builds bridges instead of walls.

Today, let your voice be an instrument of peace in your home. Even when correction is needed, wrap it in kindness. Let your gentleness be a testimony of God's grace at work in you.

CHALLENGE

Today, pay attention to your tone, not just your words.
If you feel irritation rising, lower your voice instead of raising it.
Whisper a prayer before you respond.

Notice how softness invites understanding where sharpness
once caused distance.

PRAYER

*Lord, tame my tongue and tenderize my tone. When I'm
frustrated or misunderstood, help me speak with kindness
instead of criticism. Let my words carry peace, not pride, and
healing instead of hurt.*

*Teach me to mirror Your gentleness...even when emotions rise.
May my home be filled with the calm that comes from Your
Spirit within me.*

Amen

DECREE

My words will heal, not harm.
I will clothe my tone with gentleness and grace.
Peace will follow the sound of my voice.

REFLECTION JOURNAL

How does my tone affect the mood in our home? What happens when I respond softly instead of sharply? Did I notice a moment today where gentleness diffused tension? How can I practice using softness as strength in my marriage?

A gentle tone can do what a sharp word
never will.

PHASE 2

Phase 2: Softening & Surrender (Days 8–15)

The softest hearts often carry the deepest strength.

Once awareness begins, surrender follows.
This is where transformation takes root...in the letting go.

You'll learn to release expectations, forgive faster, and respond instead of react. God will begin to peel away what's hardened so compassion can grow in its place.

These days are not about losing control but about giving it back to the One who can do far more with your marriage than striving ever could.

PHASE 2 PRAYER

Father, soften my heart where it's grown guarded. Teach me the power of gentle strength, the kind that releases rather than resists.

When I want to fix or prove, remind me to trust You with what I can't control. Help me surrender offense, unmet expectations, and my need to be right. Make my heart tender again, open to

Amen

PHASE 2 DECREE

I will surrender control and choose grace.
God's love will soften what pride has hardened.
My strength will come through humility, not striving.

RESPOND,
DON'T REACT

"A person's wisdom yields patience; it is to one's glory to
overlook an offense."

PROVERBS 19:11 (NIV)

There was a time when one wrong word from Matt could send
me straight into defense mode. If he said something in the
wrong tone or forgot something important, I'd instantly
react...sarcasm, snappy words, or shutting down completely.

I thought my reactions were justified. Atfter all, if he hadn't said
or done that, I wouldn't be upset. But one day, in the middle of
another quick flare-up, I heard that quiet conviction in my
spirit: *"Your reaction is your responsibility."*

That stopped me.
I realized I'd been living in emotional autopilot...letting every
word, action, or oversight determine my mood. But God was
inviting me to a higher way.

Instead of reacting from emotion, I could respond from peace. Instead of letting offense drive the moment, I could let the Holy Spirit lead it.

The next time tension rose, I paused and whispered a simple prayer: *"Holy Spirit, lead my response."*

It didn't mean the conversation was easy, but it was holy. Because for the first time, I was choosing response over reaction and peace over pride. I had to die to self.

REFLECTION

Reacting is instinctive. Responding is intentional. Reactions are fueled by emotion. Responses are guided by wisdom. One adds fuel to the fire; the other invites peace into the room.

Self-control isn't about suppressing feelings but rather surrendering them to the Holy Spirit.

When we react out of hurt, we defend ourselves. But when we respond with grace, we let God defend us.

You can't control what your husband says or does, but you can control how you handle it. When offense knocks today, pause long enough to decide: Will I react in emotion or respond in love?

CHALLENGE

Today, practice responding instead of reacting.
When something frustrates you, pause long enough to whisper,
"Holy Spirit, help me respond."

Give yourself permission to stay quiet for a moment before
answering. You'll be amazed at how often peace will win the
battle before a word is even spoken.

PRAYER

*Holy Spirit, help me to be slow to react and quick to respond
with grace. When my emotions rise, remind me to breathe
before I speak. Build a wall of peace around my heart so
offense can't enter easily.*

*Teach me to live led by Your Spirit, not by my feelings.
May my responses reflect Your wisdom, patience, and love.*

Amen

DECREE

I will respond with wisdom, not react from emotion.
The Holy Spirit will guide my words and guard my heart.
Self-control will be my strength and peace my reward.

REFLECTION JOURNAL

What situations tend to trigger my reactions? How did it feel to pause and respond differently today? What role did the Holy Spirit play in guiding my words or silence? How can I keep building the habit of responding with wisdom instead of reacting from emotion?

A Spirit-led response will always outshine an emotion-led reaction.

EXPECTATIONS — THE SILENT KILLER

"My grace is sufficient for you,

for My power is made perfect in weakness."

2 Corinthians 12:9 (NIV)

There was a time I believed Matt should just know.

He should know that I wanted him to plan a date. He should know that I needed a break. He should know that I was upset, even though I hadn't said a word.

And when he didn't know? I took it personally.

I'd stew in quiet frustration, convinced that his lack of awareness meant he didn't care. But one day, in the middle of one of those internal pity parties, I felt the Lord whisper, *"He's not failing you. He's just not reading a script he doesn't have."*

That truth hit hard. I realized I had been holding Matt hostage to expectations I'd never actually communicated. I was demanding mindreading instead of offering grace.

When I began voicing my needs or desires clearly, without accusation, sarcasm, or silent resentment, something shifted. Matt started responding with love and attentiveness, not because I controlled him, but because I finally invited him in.

Unspoken expectations create invisible tension. Honest communication creates connection.

REFLECTION

Expectations in marriage aren't the problem. Unrealistic or unspoken ones are.

When we silently assume our husband should think, feel, or act a certain way, we set him up to fail a test he didn't even know he was taking.

Offense often grows in the soil of unmet expectation. But grace grows in the soil of clear communication.

Today, examine your heart. Are you expecting something from your husband that you haven't expressed?

Instead of waiting for him to "just know," invite him into your needs with love and humility.

Remember, you're teammates...not opponents.

CHALLENGE

Today, notice when disappointment creeps in and trace it back
to the expectation behind it.

Ask yourself: *Did I communicate this clearly? Is this
expectation fair?*

If not, release it to God or express it calmly to your husband.
Choose clarity over assumption, and connection over
quiet resentment.

PRAYER

*Lord, help me to release the expectations that cause frustration
and offense. Teach me to communicate clearly, kindly, and
with grace.*

*When I feel unseen or disappointed, remind me that my
fulfillment comes from You first. Give me wisdom to share my
heart without blame and patience to listen without pride.*

*Let my marriage be filled with understanding instead of
assumption.*

Amen

DECREE

I release every unspoken expectation.
I choose clarity over assumption and grace over offense.
My peace is built on truth, not silent resentment.

What unspoken expectations have been stirring frustration in my marriage? How can I express my needs in a loving and respectful way? What happens when I release expectations to God instead of holding them against my husband? How does honest communication shift the atmosphere in our home?

*Unspoken expectations
become unseen offenses.*

10

DON'T TAKE IT PERSONALLY

"Love always protects, always trusts, always hopes,

always perseveres."

1 CORINTHIANS 13:7 (NIV)

I'll never forget the evening Matt came home from work unusually quiet. He barely said a word during dinner, and when I asked how his day was, his answer was short.

Instantly, my mind went into overdrive.
Did I do something wrong?
Is he upset with me?
Did I say something earlier that bothered him?

Within minutes, I had convinced myself I was the problem. But as the night went on, I felt the Holy Spirit nudge me: *"This isn't about you."*

Later, Matt shared that he'd had a stressful day at work, a deal had fallen through, and he was just mentally exhausted. He hadn't been mad at me at all.

That moment opened my eyes to how quickly I personalize things that have nothing to do with me. When I attach my worth to his mood, I let insecurity dictate my peace.

The truth is, sometimes our husbands are quiet because they're processing. Sometimes they pull back because they're burdened. And sometimes, it really has nothing to do with us.

When I learned to stop taking things personally, I found freedom and gave him space to be human without me assuming blame.

REFLECTION

Taking things personally creates unnecessary pain. It turns neutral moments into emotional battles and feeds the lie that our identity depends on someone else's behavior.

But when our peace comes from God, not from how others act, we become unshakable.

You can love your husband deeply without making his every word, tone, or silence about you.

When offense tries to whisper, *"He doesn't care,"* remind your heart, *"My worth is secure in Christ."*

When you stop absorbing every mood or misunderstanding as rejection, you'll discover a peace that no person can take away.

Today, give your husband room to be human and give yourself permission to stay rooted in truth.

CHALLENGE

Today, when your husband's tone, silence, or actions trigger insecurity, pause before assuming it's about you.

Ask God for perspective.

Pray for your husband instead of reacting to him.
At the end of the day, thank God for helping you stay grounded in grace instead of taking the bait of offense.

PRAYER

Lord, teach me to find my peace in You, not in how others treat me. When I'm tempted to take things personally, remind me that my worth is not up for debate.

Help me see my husband through eyes of compassion instead of insecurity. Give me discernment to know when to speak, when to pray, and when to simply let go.

Anchor my heart so deeply in Your love that offense has nowhere to land.

Amen

DECREE

I will not absorb what isn't mine.
My peace is anchored in Christ, not emotion.
I am free to love without fear, secure in His truth.

What situations or behaviors do I tend to take personally? How does insecurity influence my reactions? What truth about my identity can I cling to when offense whispers lies? How does releasing the need for constant reassurance bring peace to my heart and home?

*You protect your peace
when you refuse to take things personally.*

PRAY BEFORE
YOU REPLAY

"Do not be anxious about anything, but in every situation,
by prayer and petition, with thanksgiving, present your
requests to God. And the peace of God, which transcends all
understanding, will guard your hearts and your minds in
Christ Jesus."

PHILIPPIANS 4:6–7 (NIV)

There was a season when, after every argument or tense moment, I'd replay the conversation on a loop in my mind. *What I said. What he said. What I should have said.*

I'd mentally revisit every detail... his tone, his facial expression, the timing of his response, over and over again. I told myself I was processing, but really, I was fueling offense.

One morning, after replaying a small disagreement for hours, I felt that still, small voice whisper, "Have you talked to Me about it yet?"

Conviction and comfort hit all at once.
I hadn't prayed. I'd only replayed.

That day, I made a choice: before I replay, I'll pray.
Before I invite my thoughts to spiral, I'll invite God to
settle them.

And you know what happened? The heaviness lifted.
Because prayer shifts what replay magnifies. Prayer heals what
overthinking harms.

When I prayed first, God often changed my heart before He
changed the situation.

REFLECTION

Replaying keeps offense alive; prayer lays it down.
When we dwell on what went wrong, we give the enemy a
highlight reel to work with. He twists, amplifies, and adds
assumptions until something small becomes something huge.

But when we pray before we replay, we take our thoughts
captive instead of being held captive by them. Prayer clears our
perspective and invites the peace of God to take the place of
pride, pain, or defensiveness.

Every time you feel your mind starting to rehash what
happened, pause and whisper, *"Jesus, take this thought."*

You'll be amazed at how quickly He can calm what overthinking stirs up.

CHALLENGE

Today, when a frustrating moment replays in your mind, stop and pray instead.

Tell God exactly how you feel… hurt, irritated, misunderstood, and ask Him to show you what's true.

Refuse to let offense rent space in your thoughts.
Choose to release it through prayer and watch how peace follows.

PRAYER

Lord, help me to bring my thoughts to You before they take over. When I'm tempted to replay conversations, let prayer be my first response. Quiet my mind, soften my heart, and remind me that You bring clarity where confusion reigns.

Teach me to trust You more than my own interpretations. Let peace guard my thoughts and Your Spirit guide my responses.

Amen

DECREE

I will pray before I replay.

Jesus will guard my thoughts and guide my peace.

What prayer surrenders, offense cannot sustain.

REFLECTION JOURNAL

What moments or conversations do I tend to replay the most? How does replaying affect my mood, patience, or tone? What happens when I invite God into that thought instead? How can I make prayer my first response instead of my final resort?

Prayer quiets what replays
try to amplify.

GRACE IN THE
GRAY AREAS

"So then, make it your top priority to live a life of peace with
harmony in your relationships, eagerly seeking to
strengthen and encourage one another."

ROMANS 14:19 (TPT)

There was a time when I thought harmony in marriage meant
seeing everything the same way.

Same parenting style.

Same schedule preferences.

Same opinions on how the dishwasher should be loaded.

But the longer we were married, the more I realized... there's a
lot of gray in marriage. Things that don't have one clear right or
wrong answer... just two different perspectives.

Matt and I see the world differently. He's more laid-back; I'm
more structured. He wants to enjoy the moment; I want to plan
for the next one.

Even something as simple as driving somewhere highlights our differences. If we're heading to dinner, Matt will take the scenic route...windows down, music up, enjoying the view, maybe even stopping to admire the sunset. I, on the other hand, am focused on finding the fastest route with the least traffic and the best parking.

To him, the journey is part of the joy.
To me, the goal is getting there efficiently.
Neither is right or wrong... *just different.*

For years, those differences frustrated me because I saw them as flaws. But God began showing me something deeper: Our differences weren't obstacles, they were opportunities to grow in grace.

I started noticing that when I loosened my grip and gave space for his way to be different without being wrong, peace returned to our home. Grace filled the gaps where control used to live. A new kind of freedom took root.

And I realized marriage thrives not when we always agree, but when we always choose grace in the gray.

REFLECTION

Not everything needs to be corrected, fixed, or done your way. Some things just need grace.

When we let differences trigger offense, we lose the beauty of balance that God intended.

Your husband's way of thinking, doing, or leading might look different from yours and that's okay. His strengths fill your blind spots, and yours fill his.

The gray areas are where humility grows. It's where God teaches us to love without conditions and extend patience without proof.

Today, when something doesn't go your way, whisper, "Grace for the gray." You might be surprised at how much peace that one phrase invites.

CHALLENGE

Notice one area today where you and your husband naturally differ...your pace, your preferences, or your perspective. Instead of trying to change him, thank God for the balance his difference brings.

Practice responding with patience instead of pushing for your way.

PRAYER

Lord, help me to give grace in the gray areas of our marriage. When I'm tempted to correct or control, remind me that different doesn't mean wrong. Teach me to celebrate our differences as part of Your design, not as sources of frustration.

Fill our home with patience, gentleness, and humility. May our marriage reflect Your grace in every gray space.

Amen

DECREE

I choose grace where differences live.
Different is not wrong, it's refining.
Peace will lead me in every gray space.

What "gray areas" in my marriage tend to cause tension? How can I respond with grace instead of frustration? How do our differences actually strengthen our relationship? What happens when I allow space for both of us to be right in different ways?

Differences don't divide us
when grace defines us.

13

SEEING HIM
AS GOD SEES HIM

"The Lord does not look at the things people look at.
People look at the outward appearance, but the Lord looks
at the heart."

1 SAMUEL 16:7 (NIV)

There was a time when I was so focused on Matt's flaws that it clouded how I saw him. Every weakness stood out like a flashing light. The little things...his tone, his habits, his forgetfulness, became magnified until I could barely see the good anymore.

One morning, after he asked me the same question three times (making it painfully obvious he wasn't listening), I felt the Lord whisper, *"Look at him through My eyes."*

I paused.

And in that quiet moment, I imagined what God saw when He looked at Matt—not the man who accidentally got pen ink all over our comforter, but the man who worked hard to provide, who loved deeply, who carried more than he ever said out loud.

I saw a son of God.
A man chosen, redeemed, and loved.
A man under construction…just like me.

That realization softened me.
It reminded me that I wasn't called to critique him but to cover him in prayer.

When I shifted my focus from frustration to faith, everything changed…my words, my tone, and eventually, my heart.

REFLECTION

When offense creeps in, our vision narrows. We start seeing only what bothers us and miss what blesses us.

But when we ask God to help us see through His eyes, our perspective clears.

We begin to see not just our husband's flaws, but his effort… not just his shortcomings, but his potential.

You can't pray for someone and stay bitter toward them at the same time. Seeing him through God's eyes doesn't mean ignoring imperfections. It means trusting God with them.

Ask the Lord today, *"Show me who You see when You look at my husband."*

Let His vision reshape yours. When you see through heaven's lens, love flows more freely, offense loses power, and hope begins to rise again.

CHALLENGE

Today, look for one thing in your husband that reflects God's character, for example, his patience, humor, strength, loyalty, or kindness, and thank him for it out loud.

Then, write his name in your journal and ask God to show you new ways to honor and pray for him.

PRAYER

Father, help me to see my husband the way You do. When I'm tempted to fix him, remind me that You're the only One who can truly transform a heart.

Open my eyes to his strengths, his efforts, and the beauty You've placed inside him. Teach me to speak life instead of frustration and to cover him in prayer instead of criticism. Let my vision be filled with grace.

Amen

DECREE

I will see my husband through God's eyes.

I will look for his heart, not his flaws.

My love will reflect heaven's perspective, full of grace and truth.

REFLECTION JOURNAL

How have I been viewing my husband lately...through criticism or compassion? What does God see in him that I've been missing? How does prayer shift the way I see his heart? What would change in our marriage if I chose to see him through God's eyes every day?

When you see him through God's eyes,
love comes back into view.

BITE YOUR TONGUE,
BLESS INSTEAD

"Set a guard, O Lord, over my mouth; keep watch over the
door of my lips!"

PSALM 141:3 (ESV)

There was a season in my marriage when I felt like I needed to
have the last word.

If Matt said something I didn't like, I had a comeback ready.
If he was wrong, I wanted to make sure he knew it.

And if I was hurt, my words made sure he felt it too.
But one day, during a quiet time with the Lord, I came across
Psalm 141:3. I read it slowly, then prayed it out loud: *"Set a
guard over my mouth, Lord."*

I realized my tongue had been doing more damage than I
thought. Not because I was cruel, but because I spoke without
pausing. I reacted instead of responding. I corrected

instead of covering.

So I started practicing something simple but powerful: biting my tongue. When I felt that sting of irritation rise up, I'd literally close my lips and whisper, *"Bless instead."*

It felt awkward at first. My pride wanted to prove a point. But the more I stayed silent and chose to bless in prayer or with kind words, the more peace filled our home.

I learned that sometimes the most powerful words are the ones we don't say and the most healing ones are the blessings we speak instead.

REFLECTION

Your words can build or break, heal or hurt, invite peace or fuel offense. Every time you want to speak sharply, you have a choice: to bite your tongue or to bless.

Biting your tongue doesn't mean silencing your heart, it means surrendering your response. It's letting the Holy Spirit filter your words before they leave your lips.

Blessing shifts the atmosphere. When you choose to bless instead of bite, you disarm the enemy's plan to divide and invite God's presence into the moment.

Today, let your words be few and your blessings many. Speak life where your flesh wants to lash out.

CHALLENGE

Today, when you're tempted to make a sarcastic remark, correct harshly, or say something defensive...stop.

Bite your tongue, take a breath, and whisper, "Bless instead." Speak one genuine word of encouragement or pray silently for your husband instead of reacting.

PRAYER

Lord, put a guard over my mouth today.
When irritation rises, help me pause before I speak.
Let my words bring healing, not harm; blessing, not bitterness.
Fill my mouth with grace and my heart with patience.
Teach me to speak life into my husband and peace into our
home.

Amen

DECREE

I will bless instead of bite.
The Holy Spirit will guard my mouth.
My words will plant peace and pull up offense.

REFLECTION JOURNAL

When do I most often speak out of irritation instead of inspiration? How did biting my tongue and choosing blessing change today's outcome? What specific blessing or kind word can I speak over my husband daily? How does choosing silence at the right time protect peace in our marriage?

A withheld word
can become a planted blessing.

LET LOVE LEAD

"Let all that you do be done in love."

1 CORINTHIANS 16:14 (ESV)

Halfway through my 30-day challenge, I realized something unexpected. The point wasn't to become less offended, it was to become more loving.

Every pause, every prayer, every moment that I chose curiosity over criticism was really about one thing: *letting love lead.*

One morning, after a tense night of misunderstanding, I woke up with a heavy heart. I wanted to stay quiet and guarded, but the Lord whispered, *"Love first. I'll handle the rest."*

So I did something simple. I reached over, rested my hand on Matt's, and said, *"Good morning."* That's it.

But that one act broke the tension that offense was trying to build.

In that moment, I felt the Holy Spirit remind me: *Love is the differencemaker.*

It's not weakness. It's warfare that disarms pride, silences offense, and creates space for healing.

From that day forward, whenever I felt resistance rise up in me, I asked, *"What would love do here?"*

And that question changed everything.

REFLECTION

At the center of an unoffendable heart is love, not the kind that depends on someone else's behavior, but the kind that reflects Christ's heart.

Love leads with grace, even when it's undeserved.
Love listens before defending.
Love chooses peace over being right, humility over control, and forgiveness over frustration.

When love leads, offense loses its grip.
Every decision, every word, every response filtered through love becomes an act of worship.

Today, let love go first and trust that everything else will follow.

CHALLENGE

Before every interaction with your husband today, pause and ask yourself: *"What would love do?"*

Let that question guide your tone, your attitude, and your response. At the end of the day, reflect on how choosing love changed your heart and maybe even changed the atmosphere in your home.

PRAYER

Lord, help me to let love lead every thought,
word, and action today. When my flesh wants to react,
remind me to respond in love.

When my pride wants to rise, let humility take its place.
Teach me to love like You... patiently, gently, and without
condition. Let my marriage become a reflection
of Your love at work in me.

Amen

DECREE

Love will go first in me.
Peace, not pride, will set my tone.
Where love leads, offense loses.

REFLECTION JOURNAL

How does letting love lead change the way I see and respond to my husband? What areas of my heart still try to lead with control, pride, or fear? What specific moment today revealed the power of love in action? How can I make "let love lead" my daily motto in marriage?

Where love leads,
offense loses.

PHASE 3

Phase 3: Connection & Renewal (Days 16–23)
After softening comes sweetness - the fruit of grace taking root.

This phase is about rebuilding closeness. You'll rediscover gratitude, listen with empathy, and find joy in small, sacred moments.

Connection doesn't happen through perfection but through presence. These days will remind you that peace is possible again - that laughter, gentleness, and unity can return to a marriage surrendered to grace.

PHASE 3 PRAYER

Lord, restore what distance has taken. Teach me to rebuild trust through small acts of kindness and consistent grace. Renew the joy and laughter that once came easily.

Help me listen deeply, speak softly, and love intentionally. Breathe new life into our connection and let Your Spirit weave unity where offense once lived.

Amen

PHASE 3 DECREE

I will nurture connection through peace and patience.

God's Spirit will renew our love daily.

What grace restores, no offense can destroy.

16

THE BEAUTY
OF SILENCE

"The Lord will fight for you; you need only to be still."

EXODUS 14:14 (NIV)

There was a time when I thought silence meant weakness.
If I didn't speak up, how would things ever change?
If I stayed quiet, wouldn't that mean I was letting things slide?

But over time, I learned there's a difference between peaceful silence and punishing silence.

Punishing silence withdraws, walls off, and wounds. Peaceful silence pauses, prays, and protects.

One night, after a tense conversation that could've easily turned into an argument, I felt the urge to defend myself. I had all the words ready...the points, the logic, the proof. But something in me said, *"Just stop."*

So, I stayed quiet.

Not with coldness, but with calm.

I let the moment breathe.

And in that silence, something holy happened. God spoke to *me*. He reminded me that I didn't need to win every battle with words. Sometimes the most powerful thing I can do is stay still and let Him work in the unseen.

That night, peace settled where offense had been trying to grow. I discovered the beauty of silence that surrenders control to God.

REFLECTION

Silence can be sacred when it's filled with prayer instead of pride.

You don't always need to respond, explain, or correct. Sometimes, choosing silence is choosing trust... trust that God sees, knows, and will speak when it's time.

In a world that tells us to "speak our truth," God sometimes invites us to guard it instead. Not out of fear, but out of faith.

Let silence be your soft armor today.

When emotions rise, stay still long enough for peace to settle.

You'll be amazed how many storms calm themselves when words don't fuel them.

CHALLENGE

Today, resist the urge to have the last word.
When tension rises, choose silence, not the kind that punishes, but the kind that prays.

Take a deep breath and whisper, "God, You can speak louder than I can." Let your peace become your loudest response.

PRAYER

Lord, teach me the strength of silence.
When I want to defend, correct, or explain, help me to pause and trust You instead. Fill my quiet moments with Your presence, not pride.
Let my stillness create space for Your Spirit to move.
May my peace speak louder than my words today.

Amen

DECREE

I will choose peaceful silence over prideful noise.
My stillness will make space for God to speak.
His peace will fight battles my words never could.

REFLECTION JOURNAL

How do I usually respond when I feel misunderstood or criticized? What does "peaceful silence" look like for me compared to "punishing silence"? What happened today when I chose quiet trust instead of quick words? How does stillness invite God's presence into conflict?

Stillness makes room for God to speak
where your words would only stir.

FORGIVENESS
IN REAL TIME

"Don't let the sun go down while you are still angry."

EPHESIANS 4:26 (NLT)

Forgiveness used to feel like something that came after the pain...something you do once the anger fades, the apology comes, or time dulls the sting.

But God began to show me another way: forgiveness in real time.

It started during an ordinary evening when Matt said something that triggered a tender spot. My feelings were hurt, and my mind immediately started to spiral: *He should know better. He should understand how that made me feel.*

But before the offense could take root, I heard that gentle whisper: *"Forgive now."*

Not later. Not after a talk. Not after he realized it. **Now.**

So, I took a deep breath and whispered quietly, *"I forgive him."* In that instant, peace entered where pride wanted to stay. The moment softened. My tone softened. And when we did talk later, it was from love rather than resentment.

That's when I realized: forgiveness doesn't just set the offender free, it sets me free before bitterness has a chance to build.

REFLECTION

Forgiveness in real time is choosing freedom before feelings catch up. It's deciding that offense doesn't get to live in your heart...not even for a minute.

You may still feel hurt. You may still need to talk things through. But choosing forgiveness first keeps your heart clean so that healing has room to grow.

Every time you whisper, *"I forgive,"* heaven hears.
You're breaking agreement with bitterness and making space for God to work.

Forgiveness doesn't mean forgetting or excusing; it means handing the moment to God before it poisons your peace.

CHALLENGE

Today, when something small stings or irritates you, don't let it linger. Pause, breathe, and say, out loud or in your heart, *"I forgive."*

You don't need to wait for an apology or the perfect moment.

Release it in real time and watch how light your heart feels by the day's end.

PRAYER

Lord, help me to forgive in real time. When offense tries to settle in, remind me to release it before it takes root. Give me a heart quick to forgive, slow to accuse, and eager to love.

Teach me to trust that You can heal what words or timing can't. Thank You for forgiving me freely so I can forgive freely too.

Amen

DECREE

I will forgive quickly and completely.
Offense will not take root in my heart.
Grace will flow through me the moment I'm hurt.

REFLECTION JOURNAL

What small offenses am I still holding onto from today or this week? How does forgiving in the moment shift my emotions and the atmosphere? What's harder for me: saying "I forgive" or truly letting go? How can I make forgiveness a reflex instead of a reaction?

Quick forgiveness keeps offense
from taking root.

18

CHOOSING GRATITUDE
MID-CONFLICT

"Give thanks in all circumstances; for this is the will of God
in Christ Jesus for you."

It's easy to be grateful when everything feels peaceful.
But what about when your husband's tone is sharp or when
dinner's burned, the kids are loud, and you're already
stretched thin?

One evening, during my challenge, Matt and I were in the
middle of a disagreement that had been simmering all day. He
said something that hit me wrong, and I felt the familiar pull
toward offense. My mind started to gather its ammunition,
everything he'd said or done lately that added fuel to the fire.

But right in the middle of it, I felt the Holy Spirit nudge my
heart: *"Thank Me right now."*

Honestly, I didn't want to. Gratitude was the last thing on my mind. But I whispered anyway, *"Lord, thank You for this man. Thank You for his heart, even when I don't understand it."*

Something shifted. My tone softened. My anger shrank. I saw Matt not as my opponent but as my partner again.

Gratitude didn't erase the conflict but it changed me in the middle of it. And that changed everything.

REFLECTION

Gratitude is a weapon against offense. It repositions your heart from frustration to faith, from what's missing to what's still good.

When you choose gratitude mid-conflict, you break the cycle of negativity before it spirals.

You remind your soul that God is still present even in disagreement.

Gratitude doesn't deny reality; it declares hope. It says, "This moment may be hard, but God is still good. My husband is still a gift. Love is still worth choosing."

Today, let thankfulness interrupt your arguments. It's hard to stay offended when your heart is giving thanks.

CHALLENGE

When irritation or conflict rises today, stop and thank God for one thing about your husband or your marriage. Say it out loud.

You'll be surprised how fast gratitude can dissolve offense. At the end of the day, write down three things you're thankful for...even if the day was messy.

PRAYER

Lord, help me to choose gratitude even when my emotions say otherwise. When conflict rises, remind me of the blessings that haven't changed. Thank You for my husband... for his heart, his efforts, and the life we're building together.

Let thankfulness soften my tone, guard my words, and shift my perspective. May gratitude be my posture in both peace and tension.

Amen

DECREE

I will give thanks in every circumstance.
Gratitude will disarm offense and shift my focus.
Peace will guard my heart even in conflict.

REFLECTION JOURNAL

How does gratitude change the way I see my husband in the middle of frustration? What blessings do I overlook when I focus on what's wrong? What specific moment today showed me the power of thankfulness? How can I build a habit of gratitude that lasts beyond this challenge?

19

REWRITING
THE NARRATIVE

"Do not conform to the pattern of this world, but be transformed by the renewing of your mind."

ROMANS 12:2 (NIV)

There was a stretch of time when I unknowingly let offense become my narrator.

If Matt was quiet, my thoughts whispered, *He's distant again.*
If he forgot something, *He doesn't listen.*
If he was distracted, *He doesn't care.*

Before long, I wasn't reacting to reality. I was reacting to the story I'd created in my head.

One day, after stewing over something small, I felt the Holy Spirit nudge me: *"You're believing a story that isn't true."*

I paused and realized how much pain I had created by assuming motives instead of asking questions, by rehearsing frustration instead of speaking grace.

So, I began to practice rewriting the narrative.
When the enemy whispered, *He doesn't care*, I countered, *He's tired, but he still showed up.*

When the thought came, *He never helps*, I reminded myself, *He worked all day for our family.*

It didn't mean I ignored real issues, but I stopped giving power to false ones.

As my narrative changed, so did the atmosphere of our home.

REFLECTION

The story you tell yourself about your husband determines how you feel about him.

The enemy loves to twist small moments into toxic stories...stories that exaggerate, assume, and accuse.

But God invites you to renew your mind, to speak truth over the moments offense wants to distort.

When you rewrite the narrative, you're not denying your feelings but you're disciplining them. You're choosing to align your thoughts with God's truth, not your assumptions.

Today, when frustration or misunderstanding creeps in, stop and ask, *"What story am I telling myself and does it line up with God's heart?"*

You'll be amazed how quickly peace returns when your thoughts agree with truth.

CHALLENGE

Today, notice when a negative thought about your husband enters your mind, pause and replace it with truth.

Instead of *"He doesn't care,"* say *"He's doing his best."* Instead of *"He never notices,"* say *"He shows love in different ways."*

Keep rewriting until your thoughts match God's heart.

PRAYER

Lord, renew my mind and rewrite the stories I've been believing. When offense or insecurity tries to narrate my heart, remind me to listen to Your truth instead.

Help me to see my husband through grace, not suspicion. Teach me to take every thought captive and replace lies with love.

May my inner dialogue always reflect Your peace,
patience, and goodness.

Amen

DECREE

I will take every thought captive to truth.
My mind will agree with God, not assumption.
Grace will rewrite the stories offense once told.

REFLECTION JOURNAL

What false narratives do I tend to believe about my husband or our marriage? How do those thoughts affect my emotions, words, and connection? What truths can I replace them with today? How did rewriting the narrative bring peace to my heart?

When truth rewrites your thoughts,
peace rewrites your marriage.

PROTECTING
HIS REPUTATION

"Do not let any unwholesome talk come out of your mouths,
but only what is helpful for building others up."

EPHESIANS 4:29 (NIV)

For many years of my marriage, I didn't realize how casually I
spoke about Matt.

A joke here, a complaint there...nothing terrible, just little
comments about his habits or forgetfulness. Sometimes it was
with friends, sometimes even in front of the kids.

But one day, I caught the look on his face when a friend teased
him about something I had shared. His eyes dropped, and my
heart sank. I hadn't meant to embarrass him, but I did.

Later, I felt the Holy Spirit whisper, *"You can't build him up in
private and tear him down in public."*

That moment changed me. I realized that as his wife, my words have power, to protect or to expose, to honor or to humiliate. The world doesn't need to know his flaws; they need to see my faithfulness.

Now, when I feel tempted to vent or "process" something with others, I pause and ask myself, *"Would I want him speaking about me this way?"*

I've learned that one of the greatest signs of love is the choice to protect his reputation even when you're frustrated. Because honor speaks volumes, especially when no one's watching.

REFLECTION

In a world that celebrates oversharing and airing dirty laundry, protecting your husband's reputation is a radical act of love.

It doesn't mean you can't seek wise counsel or support. It means you do so with respect and discretion. You speak in ways that protect, not expose.

When you cover your husband in grace, you become a safe place for him. And where safety exists, love thrives.

Today, decide to speak words that build his reputation rather than break it. Let your loyalty be louder than your frustration, and your respect stronger than your irritation.

CHALLENGE

Today, pay attention to how you speak about your husband to friends, to family, even to your kids.

If a complaint starts to form, pause and replace it with a compliment. If you need to share a frustration, take it to God first or to a trusted, godly confidant who will point you toward unity, not division. Honor him in private and in public.

PRAYER

Lord, help me to guard my husband's reputation as fiercely as I guard my own. When I'm tempted to complain or make him the punchline, remind me that my words carry weight.

Teach me to speak honor in every conversation...both in his presence and behind his back. Let my words reflect grace, loyalty, and love that covers.

Amen

DECREE

I will honor my husband with my words.
Loyalty will lead my conversations.
My speech will protect, not expose, the man I love.

REFLECTION JOURNAL

How have I spoken about my husband this week - in front of others or online? What impact do my words have on how others see him? How can I protect his reputation while still being honest about my feelings? What would change in our marriage if my words consistently built him up?

*Your words are either a shelter
or a spotlight—choose shelter.*

WHEN HE DOESN'T NOTICE YOU

"You are the God who sees me."

GENESIS 16:13 (NIV)

It was a Friday night; the house was buzzing, dinner half-done, kids everywhere. I'd gotten dressed up...nothing fancy, just something that made me feel like *me* again.

Matt walked through the door, smiled, said a quick hi to the kids...and never said a word about how I looked.

My heart sank. I wanted to shrug it off, but the sting lingered. That quiet whisper of offense crept in: *He doesn't even notice me anymore.*

Later that evening, while folding laundry and nursing my bruised feelings, I sensed the Lord's gentle nudge: *"Before you expect him to see you, remember I see you."*

Those words wrapped around my heart like a blanket. God saw my effort, my heart, my longing to be noticed. And suddenly, I realized...I'd been trying to fill a God-sized need for affirmation with human eyes.

When Matt finally came to sit beside me, he put his arm around me and said, "You look really pretty tonight."

By then, the ache was already healed because I'd let God see me first.

REFLECTION

Feeling unseen doesn't make you needy; it makes you human. But staying there can make you bitter, and bitterness will block what God is trying to heal.

When your husband seems distracted or unaware, resist the urge to withdraw or lash out. Instead, anchor yourself in the truth that God always notices you. He sees every unseen act of love, every quiet sacrifice, every prayer you whisper while loading the dishwasher.

The more you rest in being fully seen by Him, the less validation you'll need from anyone else.

And ironically, that peace makes you even more radiant and easier for your husband to see.

CHALLENGE

Today, when you start to feel invisible, stop and whisper, *"God, You see me."*

Let that truth soothe your heart before you say or do anything else. Then, instead of waiting to be noticed, speak life into your husband...compliment him, thank him, or simply smile.

You'll find that being seen by God makes it easier to see others with love.

PRAYER

Lord, thank You for seeing me...really seeing me. When I feel overlooked or unappreciated, remind me that Your eyes are on me with love and delight.

Teach me to draw worth from You, not from being noticed. Help me to see my husband with grace, even when I feel unseen. Fill our home with gentleness and mutual honor.

Amen

DECREE

God sees me fully, even when others don't.
My worth is anchored in His gaze, not human attention.

I am seen, known, and cherished by the One who never
overlooks me.

REFLECTION JOURNAL

When do I most often feel unseen or unappreciated? How does remembering that God sees me shift my emotions? What small act of love can I offer today without needing acknowledgment? How can I create an atmosphere in our home where we both feel seen and valued?

*Being unseen by man
never means being unseen by God.*

THE MINISTRY
OF LISTENING

"To answer before listening, that is folly and shame."

PROVERBS 18:13 (NIV)

I used to think I was a great listener...until I realized I was mostly listening to respond.

When Matt would talk, I'd nod along, waiting for my turn to explain, fix, or defend.

One evening, he was sharing about something that had frustrated him at work, and halfway through, I jumped in with advice he didn't ask for.

He grew quiet.
A few minutes later, he said softly, "I just needed you to hear me." Those seven words changed me.

I realized I'd been treating conversations like problem-solving sessions instead of opportunities for connection. Matt didn't always need my input. He needed my attention. He wasn't asking for answers but instead, to be understood.

That night, I made a quiet commitment: to listen like it's ministry, to make space for his heart without interruption, judgment, or correction.

Because sometimes, the most healing thing you can say is nothing at all.

REFLECTION

Listening is love in action.
It's choosing humility over hurry, empathy over ego, presence over performance.

When you really listen...to understand, not to reply, you honor the heart behind the words. You say, *"I see you. You matter."*

Your husband may not always communicate perfectly, but when he feels heard, he'll open up more.

Listening softens hearts, builds trust, and creates safety, the kind where love can thrive.

Today, give your husband the gift of full attention.
You don't need to fix him. Just hear him. That's holy work.

CHALLENGE

Practice listening without interrupting.
When your husband talks, stop what you're doing, look at him, and give him your full attention.

If you feel the urge to offer advice, ask instead, *"Do you want me to listen or help?"*

Let your presence speak louder than your words.

PRAYER

Lord, teach me to listen with compassion and patience. Quiet the noise in my mind so I can hear with my heart. Help me resist the urge to interrupt, correct, or defend.

Let my ears become instruments of peace, and my silence a safe space for connection. Thank You for always listening to me with love. Help me extend that same grace to my husband.

Amen

DECREE

I will listen to understand, not to reply.
My silence will create safety; my attention will build trust.
Every moment I truly hear becomes holy ground.

REFLECTION JOURNAL

How often do I listen to understand rather than respond? What happens when I slow down and give my husband my full attention? How does listening change the tone and trust in our conversations? What can I do to create a safe space for him to share his heart?

Listening creates the safety
where hearts learn to open.

23

HUMILITY HEALS

"Everyone should be quick to listen, slow to speak and slow
to become angry."

There was a moment early in my 30-day challenge when I felt
completely justified in my offense. Matt had said something
careless, and I was hurt. I replayed the words, rehearsed my
response, and was fully prepared to prove my point.

But before I could, I felt the Holy Spirit whisper,
"Are you more interested in being right or being healed?"

Ouch.

That question cut straight through my pride. I realized I wanted
victory more than unity. I wanted to defend myself instead of
invite peace.

So, I took a deep breath, humbled myself, and simply said, "I'm
sorry for my part in this."

It wasn't easy but what happened next felt like a miracle. The tension broke. Matt softened. We talked instead of argued.

That moment taught me something I'll never forget: humility doesn't make you small, it makes you strong enough to love through pain. It opens the door for healing to walk in.

REFLECTION

Humility is the posture of a healed heart.
It doesn't need to win, prove, or control. It trusts God to handle what pride tries to protect.

When you choose humility, you disarm offense. You make it impossible for pride to fuel division.

Pride says, *"You owe me."*
Humility says, *"God's grace is enough for both of us."*

Humility isn't about taking the blame, it's about taking responsibility for your own heart. It's what turns conflict into connection and wounds into wisdom.

Today, if you feel offended, ask yourself: *"What would humility do here?"*

You'll almost always find peace waiting on the other side.

CHALLENGE

Today, if tension arises, take the humble road first.
Be the first to soften your tone, the first to apologize, or the first
to pray.

Watch how quickly humility can dissolve what offense tries
to build.

PRAYER

*Lord, clothe me with humility today. When pride whispers that
I'm right, remind me that You call me to love. Help me lay
down my defenses and pick up grace instead.*

*Let my humility invite Your healing into my heart and home.
Make me quick to apologize, slow to accuse, and eager to
forgive.*

Amen

DECREE

I choose humility over pride and healing over being right.
My softness invites God's strength.
Grace will speak louder than my need to win.

REFLECTION JOURNAL

What situations make it hardest for me to choose humility? How does pride show up in my reactions or tone? What did humility produce in my heart (or marriage) today? How can I make humility my default posture instead of my last resort?

*Humility builds bridges
pride tried to burn.*

PHASE 4

Phase 4: Strength & Legacy (Days 24–30)
Unshakable love is the fruit of the surrendered heart.

By now, you've walked through awareness, softened what was hard, and rebuilt what was broken. This final phase is about protecting what God has restored.

You'll learn how to keep peace, how to love without conditions, how to guard your heart without closing it off, and how to live from a posture of unoffendable grace.

This is the legacy phase—the one that echoes into your family, your children, and generations to come.

PHASE 4 PRAYER

Father, thank You for the work You've done in my heart.
Help me protect this peace You've built within me.
Let my responses, my tone, and my love reflect the strength
that comes from walking closely with You.

Use my marriage as a testimony of grace for my family, my
children, and the generations to come. Let my legacy be one of

Amen

PHASE 4 DECREE

I will guard my peace and protect my legacy.
God's grace will be my strength and my song.
My love will endure because it's rooted in Him.

GUARDING YOUR HEART WITHOUT HARDENING IT

"Above all else, guard your heart, for everything you do flows from it."

PROVERBS 4:23 (NIV)

For a long time, my way of guarding my heart was by building walls.

If Matt said something that hurt me, I'd shut down.
If we disagreed, I'd withdraw.
If I felt misunderstood, I'd protect myself with silence or distance.

I told myself I was "guarding my peace," but really I was hardening my heart.

One day, during a quiet moment of prayer, I felt the Lord say, *"Misty, I asked you to guard your heart, not close it."*

Those words brought tears. I realized that in trying to protect myself from pain, I was also blocking the flow of love. My heart had become safe, but sealed.

So I asked God to teach me how to guard His way...to stay soft but wise, open but discerning.

Now, when offense tries to build a wall, I picture a gate instead. A heart with gates can let love in and send offense out. That's what true guarding looks like.

REFLECTION

Guarding your heart isn't about isolation. It's about intention. It's not shutting people out; it's filtering what gets to stay.

A hardened heart blocks everything...hurt and healing alike. A guarded heart welcomes truth, grace, and love while keeping out lies, bitterness, and pride.

You can be kind without being walked on.
You can be soft without being naïve.
You can guard your heart without closing it.

Ask the Holy Spirit to help you discern when to let things in and when to release them.

The goal isn't to be untouchable. It's to stay *unoffendable.*

CHALLENGE

Today, notice when you feel tempted to withdraw or wall off emotionally.

Instead of shutting down, pause and pray, *"God, help me guard this moment with grace."* Let Him show you whether it's time to speak truth, offer forgiveness, or simply stay still.

Keep your heart soft and your peace protected.

PRAYER

Lord, teach me how to guard my heart without hardening it. Help me stay soft and loving, even when I'm hurt. Give me discernment to know what to hold onto and what to release.

Protect me from bitterness and self-protection that shuts out love. Let my heart remain open to You, steady, secure, and safe in Your peace.

Amen

DECREE

I will guard my heart with grace, not walls.
Love will flow freely through the gates of discernment.
My softness is my strength, and peace is my protection.

REFLECTION JOURNAL

When I'm hurt, do I tend to harden or stay open? How does self-protection show up in my marriage? What does a "guarded but soft" heart look like in daily life? How did choosing grace instead of distance change my day today?

*A guarded heart stays soft
when grace holds the gate.*

PEACE OVER
PROVING YOUR POINT

"Encourage one another and build each other up."

1 THESSALONIANS 5:11 (NIV)

It started as a small disagreement... the kind that should've ended in five minutes. But I was determined to be understood. I repeated my point. I clarified. I restated.

And somewhere between "you're not listening" and "that's not what I said," the conversation turned into a competition.

By the end, neither of us felt heard. We both just felt tired.

Later, while replaying the conversation in my mind, I sensed the Lord whisper, *"You won the argument, but you lost your peace."*

That gentle conviction cut deep.

Because I realized that every time I fight to be right more than I fight to protect peace, I end up creating distance instead of connection.

The truth is, peace and pride can't coexist.
And choosing peace isn't weakness; it's wisdom.

That night, I went back to Matt, took his hand, and said, "I don't want to be *right*; I want us to be okay."

The moment I let go of my need to prove, peace came rushing back in.

REFLECTION

You can be right and still be wrong in how you handle it.
You can win an argument and lose intimacy in the process.

Peace doesn't mean silence; it means surrender.
It's choosing love over logic, humility over ego, connection over control.

Being a peacemaker doesn't mean you stop caring about truth.
It means you trust God to defend it for you.
Your peace is too precious to trade for a temporary win.

Today, choose peace. Let go of the need to prove your point and let God prove His faithfulness instead.

CHALLENGE

Today, if a disagreement arises, pause and ask yourself, *"What matters more, being right or being close?"*

If the answer is closeness, let peace lead the way.
You don't have to prove your point to prove your love.

PRAYER

Lord, help me value peace more than being right.
When pride rises and I feel the urge to defend myself, remind me that You are my defender.

Teach me to let go of arguments that steal joy and unity.
Let my words bring calm, not chaos, and let my heart rest in Your peace.

Amen

DECREE

I will choose peace over pride, connection over control.
My calm will carry more power than any argument.
Where peace leads, God's presence abides.

REFLECTION JOURNAL

What triggers my need to "prove my point" in conversations? How does pride affect my tone and ability to listen? What happened today when I chose peace instead of pushing to be right? How can I make peace my priority in every interaction?

Peace wins battles
pride should never enter.

26

SPEAK LIFE

"The tongue has the power of life and death, and those who love it will eat its fruit."

PROVERBS 18:21 (NIV)

There was a season when I didn't realize how much power my words carried. I'd say things like, "You never listen," or "You always forget," without thinking twice.

They weren't said in anger, just in exasperation. But over time, I noticed how Matt's shoulders would drop a little lower each time.

One day, while reading Proverbs, that verse about the power of the tongue stopped me in my tracks. I felt God gently say, *"Your words are planting seeds. What kind of harvest do you want to grow?"*

That image hit me hard.

Because I realized I'd been scattering frustration and then

wondering why joy wasn't growing.

So, I started paying attention...not just to what I said, but to the atmosphere my words created.

I began intentionally speaking life into Matt, even in the small things:
"Thank you for helping."
"I love how hard you work."
"I'm proud of you."

The change was almost immediate. His confidence grew, our connection deepened, and peace became the new tone in our home.

Words are powerful. They either build walls or plant gardens. Now, I try to plant beauty everywhere I speak.

REFLECTION

Every word you speak is a seed.
You're either sowing life or scattering weeds.

The words you speak over your husband can shape how he sees himself and how safe he feels in your presence. When your words are filled with love, encouragement, and respect, you create a home where hearts can grow.

Speaking life doesn't mean ignoring flaws. It means calling out potential.

It's believing the best, even when you don't see it yet.
It's choosing to speak to who he's becoming, not about who he's been.

Today, ask yourself: *Are my words healing or hurting? Building or breaking?*

Choose to be a voice that breathes life, not one that drains it.

CHALLENGE

Today, speak three intentional words of life over your husband. They can be compliments, prayers, or affirmations—big or small. Notice how the atmosphere shifts when you choose encouragement over correction.

Keep watering those words daily, and watch what grows.

PRAYER

Lord, set a guard over my mouth and fill it with words that give life. Help me speak with kindness, wisdom, and grace. When I'm tempted to criticize, remind me that my words can create change without crushing spirit.

Teach me to speak life into my husband, my home, and myself.
Let my voice echo Your love in everything I say.

Amen

DECREE

I will plant life with my tongue.
My words will build, not break.
Encouragement will be the atmosphere of my home.

REFLECTION JOURNAL

What kinds of words do I tend to speak most often—critical or lifegiving? How did my husband respond when I chose to encourage him today? What does it feel like to use my voice to bless instead of criticize? How can I make "speaking life" a daily rhythm in my marriage?

Every word you speak
becomes the atmosphere you live in.

REST FROM RESENTMENT

"Come to me, all you who are weary and burdened, and I will give you rest."

MATTHEW 11:28 (NIV)

There was a season when I didn't realize how tired I was...not from work or parenting, but from carrying resentment.

It wasn't one big offense but rather a hundred little ones I never fully released.

Every unmet expectation, every forgotten "thank you," every careless word, I tucked them away in my heart like invisible stones.

Eventually, it started to show.
I was short-tempered, distant, and emotionally drained.
One morning, during prayer, I heard the Lord whisper,
"You're tired because you're carrying things I never asked you

to hold."

I broke down right there. I realized I'd been clinging to resentment like a security blanket, afraid that letting go meant I was okay with what happened.

But forgiveness isn't saying it was okay. It's saying I won't carry it anymore.

That day, I released it all: the small slights, the big frustrations, the unspoken disappointments.

And for the first time in a long time, I could breathe again. That's what rest feels like.

REFLECTION

Resentment is heavy. It quietly accumulates until it steals your joy and hardens your heart.

But you were never meant to live weighed down by what someone else did or didn't do.

Forgiveness brings freedom, but letting go of resentment brings rest. It's the deep exhale that says, "God, You're the Judge, not me. I release this to You."

You don't have to revisit every hurt or fix every detail.

Just surrender it again and again if needed.

Each time you release, your soul rests a little more in grace. Today, choose rest over resentment. God's peace is waiting for you to set your burdens down.

CHALLENGE

Take a few quiet minutes today to sit with God and name what you've been holding onto.

Whisper, "I release this to You."
Then, take a deep breath and let it go.

If it tries to come back, repeat the process. Rest is a rhythm, not a one-time release.

PRAYER

Lord, I'm tired of carrying the weight of resentment. Help me release every hurt and disappointment I've been holding. Teach me to rest in Your grace, not my grievances.

When old pain tries to resurface, remind me that You are my healer and my defender. Let forgiveness flow freely through me, restoring peace to my heart and home.

Amen

DECREE

I lay down resentment and receive rest.

I release what I cannot carry to Jesus.

My heart will breathe in grace and exhale peace.

REFLECTION JOURNAL

What resentment have I been quietly holding onto? How has it affected my peace, tone, or closeness with my husband? What does rest feel like when I finally surrender it? How can I make releasing resentment part of my daily walk with God?

28

LOVE WITHOUT
A HOOK

"And walk in love, as Christ loved us and gave himself up
for us a fragrant offering and sacrifice to God."

EPHESIANS 5:2 (ESV)

There was a season when I didn't realize how tired I was...not
from work or parenting, but from carrying resentment.

It wasn't one big offense but rather a hundred little ones I never
fully released.

Every unmet expectation, every forgotten "thank you," every
careless word, I tucked them away in my heart like invisible
stones.

Eventually, it started to show.
I was short-tempered, distant, and emotionally drained.
One morning, during prayer, I heard the Lord whisper,
"You're tired because you're carrying things I never

asked you to hold."

I broke down right there. I realized I'd been clinging to resentment like a security blanket, afraid that letting go meant I was okay with what happened.

But forgiveness isn't saying it was okay. It's saying I won't carry it anymore.

That day, I released it all: the small slights, the big frustrations, the unspoken disappointments.

And for the first time in a long time, I could breathe again. That's what rest feels like.

REFLECTION

Resentment is heavy. It quietly accumulates until it steals your joy and hardens your heart.

But you were never meant to live weighed down by what someone else did or didn't do.

Forgiveness brings freedom, but letting go of resentment brings rest. It's the deep exhale that says, "God, You're the Judge, not me. I release this to You."

You don't have to revisit every hurt or fix every detail.

Just surrender it again and again if needed.

Each time you release, your soul rests a little more in grace. Today, choose rest over resentment. God's peace is waiting for you to set your burdens down.

CHALLENGE

Take a few quiet minutes today to sit with God and name what you've been holding onto.

Whisper, "I release this to You."
Then, take a deep breath and let it go.

If it tries to come back, repeat the process. Rest is a rhythm, not a one-time release.

PRAYER

Lord, I'm tired of carrying the weight of resentment. Help me release every hurt and disappointment I've been holding. Teach me to rest in Your grace, not my grievances.

When old pain tries to resurface, remind me that You are my healer and my defender. Let forgiveness flow freely through me, restoring peace to my heart and home.

Amen

DECREE

I lay down resentment and receive rest.

I release what I cannot carry to Jesus.

My heart will breathe in grace and exhale peace.

REFLECTION JOURNAL

What resentment have I been quietly holding onto? How has it affected my peace, tone, or closeness with my husband? What does rest feel like when I finally surrender it? How can I make releasing resentment part of my daily walk with God?

29

GRACE ON REPEAT

"His mercies never come to an end; they are new every morning."

After weeks of trying to pause, pray, and choose peace, I remember waking up one morning thinking, I shouldn't still be struggling with offense.

But then Matt said something offhand, and there it was again... the sting, the sigh, the temptation to snap back.

I felt discouraged until the Lord whispered, "Grace isn't a one-time gift. It's a daily refill."

That simple truth set me free. Because if God's mercies are new every morning, then mine can be too.

Now, when I fall short, I start over.
When offense tries to creep back in, I whisper, "Grace again."

It's not failure, it's formation.

Every repetition rewires my heart to respond more like Jesus.

Grace on repeat isn't weakness. It's training for strength.

REFLECTION

Growth doesn't mean perfection. It means persistence. Choosing grace again today doesn't cancel yesterday's progress; it cements it.

Grace on repeat looks like forgiving again, softening again, apologizing again, loving again.

It's the steady beat that keeps your marriage alive and your spirit aligned with God's heart.

Every new sunrise is another invitation:
Start over. Try again. Grace is still here.

Let that truth wash over you today. No matter how many times you've stumbled, grace still says, "We begin again."

CHALLENGE

If frustration rises today, don't count it as failure but rather another chance to practice grace.

Say it aloud: "Grace again."

Then choose one small action of love to reset the moment; a soft tone, a kind word, a fresh start.

PRAYER

Lord, thank You that Your mercy never runs out on me. Teach me to extend that same grace over and over without growing weary.

When I feel frustrated or ashamed of my reactions, remind me that I'm still learning love. Let my marriage become a place where grace never stops flowing.

Amen

DECREE

I will press reset with grace again.
His mercies renew me daily; mine will too.
Progress, not perfection, will mark my love.

Teach me to speak life into my husband, my home, and myself.

Let my voice echo Your love in everything I say.

Amen

DECREE

I will plant life with my tongue.

My words will build, not break.

Encouragement will be the atmosphere of my home.

What moments today reminded me that I still need grace? How does giving grace freely help me receive it more easily? What changes when I see grace as a rhythm, not a rescue? Where do I need to press "repeat" on forgiveness or patience right now?

When grace becomes your rhythm,
offense loses its grip.

30

UNOFFENDABLE LOVE

"And over all these virtues put on love, which binds them all
together in perfect unity."

When I first started this challenge, I thought the goal was to stop
getting offended.

But somewhere along the way, I realized it was never just about
that. *It was about learning to love like Jesus.*

To love when it's inconvenient. To love when you don't feel seen.
To love when your pride wants to argue and your heart wants
to retreat.

There was a morning toward the end of my own 30-day journey
when Matt said something that, a month before, would've set me
off instantly.

But this time, I just smiled.

Not because I'd stopped caring, but because I was finally free.

Free from needing to control, correct, or defend.
Free from keeping score.
Free from offense.

And in that quiet moment, I realized: *This is unoffendable love.*
The kind of love that flows from a heart so rooted in grace that
no word, tone, or circumstance can shake it loose.

There's absolutely nothing like it.

REFLECTION

Unoffendable love doesn't mean you'll never feel hurt.
It means you've learned what to do with the hurt when it comes.

You bring it to Jesus instead of your temper.
You respond with peace instead of pride.

You love anyway, not because it's easy, but because it's *eternal.*

This is the love that changes homes, heals marriages, and
softens generations. It's love that looks like patience,
forgiveness, gratitude, and grace...over and over again.

You didn't just complete a 30-day challenge; you began a
lifelong rhythm of choosing love when offense knocks.

And that choice will ripple through your home for years to come.

CHALLENGE

Today, celebrate how far you've come.
Write down three ways your heart has changed since starting this journey.

Then, ask God to show you one small way to keep growing in unoffendable love, because this isn't the end. It's the beginning of a new way of living.

PRAYER

Lord, thank You for teaching me the beauty of unoffendable love. Thank You for changing me from the inside out...one pause, one prayer, one act of grace at a time.

Help me carry this posture beyond these 30 days, into every season of my marriage and life. Let my love reflect Yours...steady, merciful, and unshakable.

May my words build, my patience protect, and my heart remain soft in every storm.

Amen

DECREE

I put on unoffendable love.

Peace will rule my responses.

Rooted in grace, I will not be shaken.

REFLECTION JOURNAL

What have I learned about my heart through these 30 days? How has choosing love over offense changed the atmosphere of my marriage? In what areas do I still want to grow in patience, humility, and grace? What does it mean to me to be an "Unoffendable Wife"?

Unoffendable love is the fruit
of every surrendered moment.

FINAL ENCOURAGEMENT

You've walked through 30 days of surrender, softening, and strength. You've chosen peace over being right, humility over pride, grace over grudges.

And you've discovered that unoffendable love isn't about perfection, it's about presence.

Every pause.
Every prayer.
Every moment you chose love over offense was holy ground.

Keep walking in that grace.
Your marriage, and the generations watching, will taste the fruit of your faithfulness.

Beyond
THE 30 DAYS

You did it.
Thirty days of choosing love over offense, grace over reaction,
humility over pride.

But more than finishing a challenge, you've begun a
transformation. Because *The Unoffendable Wife* isn't a title you
earn - it's a heart you cultivate, one surrendered choice at a
time.

Real life will still test you. There will be days when irritation
rises quicker than you'd like and conversations that stretch your
patience. And that's okay. Growth isn't perfection; it's progress
that keeps showing up.

Every pause before a pounce, every whispered prayer, every
time you choose peace instead of proving... those are victories.
They're bricks in the foundation of a home built on grace.

So, keep tending this posture.
When offense knocks, open the door with compassion.
When frustration flares, breathe before you speak.
When words feel heavy, let silence and love carry them instead.

You've learned to see your husband through the eyes of grace, to protect your peace, and to let love lead. Now keep walking that out, not for thirty days, but for a lifetime.

And remember: God is not only refining your marriage... He's revealing Himself through it. Every act of grace, every gentle response, every surrendered moment is a reflection of His heart in yours.

The unoffendable wife isn't perfect.
She's simply anchored... rooted in love, covered in mercy, and filled with peace that passes understanding.

You've become that woman.
Now carry her into every tomorrow.

PRAYER OF COMPLETION

Lord, thank You for walking beside me through this 30-day journey. Thank You for softening what was hard, healing what was heavy, and teaching me to love like You.

Help me live as an unoffendable wife, not by willpower, but by Your Spirit. Let my home reflect Your peace, my words reflect Your heart, and my life reflect Your love.

Amen

ONGOING PRACTICE

• Keep a small Grace Journal where you record daily moments of love, patience, or growth.

• Revisit any of these 30 days whenever you feel offense trying to sneak back in.

• Share what God has done, your story may become someone else's healing.

GROUP STUDY GUIDE

Weekly Gathering Guides

If you're walking this journey in community, the following pages are designed to support weekly gatherings through reflection, discussion, and prayer.

These guides are meant to gently hold space for the work God is doing among you, without rushing it or forcing outcomes.

They're intended as a companion to the daily readings, not a replacement, offering space to process, pray, and encourage one another as grace unfolds together.

I didn't tell Matt. I didn't mark it on the calendar or announce it like some grand challenge. It was simply a quiet whisper from the Lord: *Lay down your reactions and let Me teach you peace.*

WEEKLY GATHERING GUIDES

Week 1: Orientation & Foundation

Theme: Creating Safety, Setting Intention Read:

• Letter to the Reader

• A Gentle Note on Safety and Grace

• Introduction

• Prologue

• How to Use This Book

Opening Reflection: Before transformation begins, the heart needs safety. This week is about slowing down, settling in, and remembering that grace, not performance, sets the pace for this journey.

Group Discussion

1. What drew you to this journey in this season?
2. What does a "softer heart" look like for you personally?
3. Where do you feel pressure to perform or prove in marriage—or even here?
4. What would it look like to show up honestly instead of perfectly?
5. What do you need in order to feel safe engaging this process?

Practice Focus for the Week: Release pressure. Begin each day with this simple prayer: *"Lord, I'm willing. Meet me here."*

Closing Prayer

Lord, thank You for bringing us together.
Help us lay down expectations and open our hearts with
honesty and humility. Let this be a space marked by safety,
grace, and Your presence.

Amen

Week 2: Awareness & Reflection

Theme: Pause Before You Pounce

Read: Days 1–7

Key Scripture: James 1:19

Opening Reflection: Awareness is the doorway to change. Before peace can grow, we have to notice what's stealing it. This week invites us to become honest about our reactions, tone, assumptions, and inner dialogue, not with shame, but with grace.

Group Discussion

1. What reactions or patterns have you begun to notice?
2. Where do you tend to "pounce" the fastest...tone, sarcasm, silence, defensiveness?
3. What surprised you about your responses this week?

1. How has keeping score or needing to be right affected peace in your marriage?
2. What happens when you pause, even for a few seconds?
3. Where do you sense God inviting awareness rather than correction?

Practice Focus for the Week: Practice the pause. When irritation rises, breathe before responding and whisper: *"Holy Spirit, lead my response."*

Closing Prayer

Lord, thank You for meeting us in awareness, not shame. Help us notice what You're ready to heal. Teach us to pause before we pounce and invite You into the space between emotion and response.

Amen

Week 3: Softening & Surrender

Theme: Respond, Don't React

Read: Days 8–15

Key Scripture: Proverbs 19:11

Opening Reflection: Surrender isn't giving up, it's giving over. This week is about releasing control, expectations, and emotional autopilot.

Group Discussion

1. What expectations have you been carrying silently?
2. How do unmet expectations tend to show up in your reactions?
3. What conversations or moments do you tend to replay?
4. How does prayer shift your thought life when offense tries to settle in?
5. Where has grace begun softening something that once felt hard?
6. What does surrender look like practically in your marriage right now?

Practice Focus for the Week: Pray before you replay. When a thought loops, pause and say: *"Jesus, take this thought."*

Closing Prayer

Father, soften what pride has hardened.
Help us surrender control and trust You with what we cannot fix. Teach us to respond from peace instead of reacting from emotion.

Amen

Week 4: Connection & Renewal

Theme: Restoring Closeness Through Grace

Read: Days 16–23

Key Scripture: Proverbs 18:13

Opening Reflection: Connection doesn't come from perfection, it comes from presence. This week invites us to listen deeply, forgive quickly, and choose humility.

Group Discussion

1. What helps you feel most connected in your marriage?
2. How does gratitude shift the atmosphere during conflict?
3. What does "forgiveness in real time" look like for you?
4. Where has humility healed something pride once fueled?
5. How does being fully seen by God change the way you show up?
6. What has listening...really listening, revealed to you?

Practice Focus for the Week: Practice listening without fixing. Ask: *"Do you want me to listen or help?"*

Closing Prayer

Lord, restore what distance has taken.
Teach us to listen with compassion, forgive quickly, and love humbly.

Renew joy, trust, and closeness through Your Spirit.

Amen

Week 5: Strength & Legacy

Theme: Living Unoffendably

Read: Days 24–30

Key Scripture: Colossians 3:14

Opening Reflection: This week isn't about finishing strong, it's about living anchored. Unshakable love is built through daily grace, not perfect behavior.

Group Discussion

1. What has changed in your heart over these weeks?
2. What does guarding your heart without hardening it look like now?
3. Where have words of life shifted your home's atmosphere?
4. What does "love without a hook" mean for you?
5. How has grace on repeat freed you?
6. What does being an "unoffendable wife" mean to you today?

Practice Focus for the Week: Choose peace over proving and love over outcome.

Lord, thank You for the work You've done in us.
Help us protect the peace You've restored and carry this
posture into every season. Let our marriages reflect Your grace
for generations to come.

Amen

Week 6: Reflection, Integration & Blessing

Theme: Carrying the Posture Forward

Read:

- Final Encouragement
- Beyond the 30 Days
- Prayer of Completion
- Epilogue

Opening Reflection: This week is not about ending, it's about becoming. We pause to notice what God has done, give thanks, and anchor new rhythms of grace.

Group Discussion

1. What has changed in your heart since beginning this journey?
2. Where do you see grace on repeat in your life now?

1. What practices do you want to carry forward intentionally?
2. How has your definition of peace shifted?
3. What does it mean for offense to no longer have a home?

Practice Focus for the Week: Name what God has done. Write one sentence that begins with: *"Over these six weeks, God has shown me..."*

Closing Blessing

Lord, seal what You have begun.
Help us carry softened hearts, guarded peace, and grace-filled love into every season ahead. May our homes reflect Your gentleness and our lives reflect Your heart.

Amen

Final Thought

You are living proof that love can
transform.
That peace can protect.
That humility can heal.

You are an unoffendable wife.
Not because you never stumble, but
because every time you do, you
choose grace again.

JOIN THE MOVEMENT

If this journey has spoken to your heart, share your story!
Use **#TheUnoffendableWife** or connect with me at
mistyparenzan.com.

I love hearing how God is softening hearts, restoring peace, and
rewriting marriages with grace. Together, we're building a
community of women learning to love like Jesus - unoffendably,
wholeheartedly, and with enduring peace.

EPILOGUE

When Offense No Longer Has a Home

Before January 2021, we were always the couple everyone thought had it all together. Compared to most, our marriage looked strong: fun, connected, intentional, and full of love. And in many ways, it truly was. But looking back now, I can see that what we had then is nothing compared to what we share today.

Once I quit being unpleasant toward Matt, once I chose to pause before pouncing and humility over pride, something beautiful began to happen. He changed too.

Today, he treats me like a queen. I have never felt more seen, loved, or heard than I do now. There's a sweetness in the way we communicate, a lightness in our laughter, and a depth in our intimacy that only grace could have created.

Because offense is toxic.
It sneaks in quietly through little irritations, unmet expectations, or careless words, and begins to close our spirits one layer at a time. In an effort to protect ourselves from getting hurt, we build walls around our hearts. But those same walls

that keep pain out also keep love out.

Without Christ softening our hearts, selfishness and pride take over. Our hearts harden little by little until indifference settles in where intimacy once lived. Offense is the hidden marriage destroyer. It does its damage long before you realize what's been lost.

But when you decide that offense no longer has a home in your marriage, everything changes. You begin to see your spouse through grace-colored lenses. You stop keeping score. You learn to laugh again, to listen again, to love again.

The enemy still tries to whisper in my ear, reminding me of the things I could be irritated about or the ways Matt might disappoint me, but those whispers have lost their power. I know who I am now, and I know Who holds our marriage together.

When offense loses its home, love moves back in.
And what's left is something far more beautiful than "perfect."
It's peaceful. It's safe. It's holy.

And remember…He is *always* there.

the
UNOFFENDABLE WIFE

She doesn't love perfectly, but she loves persistently.
She pauses before she pounces, prays before she reacts,
and forgives before resentment takes root.

She's learned that peace is worth more than pride,
and grace is stronger than being right.
Her heart is guarded but not hardened,
her words soft but full of truth.

She sees her husband not through flaws,
but through the eyes of the One who redeems.
She loves without a hook, serves without applause,
and starts again with grace on repeat.

Because the unoffendable wife isn't a woman
who never feels hurt.
She's a woman who refuses to stay there.

Her strength is surrender, her weapon is love,
and her legacy... is peace.

SCRIPTURE INDEX

PHASE 1
Orientation & Foundation

Day 1: James 1:19 (NIV)

Day 2: Philippians 4:5 (NIV)

Day 3: 1 Thessalonians 5:11 (NIV)

Day 4: 1 Corinthians 13:5 (NIV)

Day 5: Matthew 5:9 (ESV)

Day 6: Philippians 4:8 (ESV)

Day 7: Proverbs 15:1 (NIV)

PHASE 2
Softening & Surrender

Day 8: Proverbs 19:11 (NIV)

Day 9: 2 Corinthians 12:9 (NIV)

Day 10: 1 Corinthians 13:7 (NIV)

Day 11: Philippians 4:6–7 (NIV)

Day 12: Romans 14:19 (TPT)

Day 13: 1 Samuel 16:7 (NIV)

Day 14: Psalm 141:3 (ESV)

Day 15: 1 Corinthians 16:14 (ESV)

PHASE 3
Connection & Renewal

Day 16: Exodus 14:14 (NIV)

Day 17: Ephesians 4:26 (NLT)

Day 18: 1 Thessalonians 5:18 (ESV)

Day 19: Romans 12:2 (NIV)

Day 20: Ephesians 4:29 (NIV)

Day 21: Genesis 16:13 (NIV)

Day 22: Proverbs 18:13 (NIV)

Day 23: 1 Peter 5:5 (NIV)

PHASE 4
Strength & Legacy

Day 24: Proverbs 4:23 (NIV)

Day 25: Colossians 3:15 (NIV)

Day 26: Proverbs 18:21 (NIV)

Day 27: Matthew 11:28 (NIV)

Day 28: Ephesians 5:2 (ESV)

Day 29: Lamentations 3:22–23 (ESV)

Day 30: Colossians 3:14 (NIV)

30 Daily Decrees for
The Unoffendable Wife

(Reflective Edition)

Day 1 — Pause Before You Pounce

I will pause before I pounce.

My words will serve peace, not pride.

The Holy Spirit will lead my reactions and guard my tone.

When I slow down, I make space for peace to lead and love to win.

Day 2 — Choose Curiosity Over Criticism

I choose curiosity over criticism.

I will look for understanding instead of fault.

Grace will open doors where judgment once closed them.

Asking "why" instead of assuming "how dare you" keeps my heart soft and safe.

Day 3 — See His Effort, Not His Error

I will see my husband's heart before his habits.

Gratitude will be my lens, not correction.

Love will cover what perfection cannot.

Seeing his heart reminds me that love grows best in grace, not control.

Day 4 — Release the Scorecard

I lay down the need to keep score.

Grace wins every time.

My marriage will be marked by mercy, not math.

When I stop counting wrongs, I start multiplying peace.

Day 5 — Choose Reconciliation Over Being Right

I will pursue peace over pride.

Connection matters more than control.

Reconciliation will be the victory I fight for.

Winning hearts matters more than winning arguments.

Day 6 — What You Feed Grows

I will feed gratitude, not grievance.

My thoughts will water peace, not offense.

What I nurture in my heart will flourish in my home.

Whatever I focus on will grow, so I'll choose what's life-giving.

Day 7 — The Power of Soft Answers

My words will heal, not harm.

I will clothe my tone with gentleness and grace.

Peace will follow the sound of my voice.

Gentleness is not weakness — it's strength under the Spirit's control.

Day 8 — Respond, Don't React

I will respond with wisdom, not react from emotion.

The Holy Spirit will guide my words and guard my heart.

Self-control will be my strength and peace my reward.

Every pause becomes an invitation for God to enter.

Day 9 — Expectations: The Silent Killer

I release every unspoken expectation.

I choose clarity over assumption and grace over offense.

My peace is built on truth, not silent resentment.

Honest communication plants peace where assumptions once grew.

Day 10 — Don't Take It Personally

I will not absorb what isn't mine.

My peace is anchored in Christ, not emotion.

I am free to love without fear, secure in His truth.

When I stop personalizing everything, I start protecting my peace.

Day 11 — Pray Before You Replay

I will pray before I replay.

Jesus will guard my thoughts and guide my peace.

What prayer surrenders, offense cannot sustain.

Prayer replaces replay — it invites peace where pride once lived.

Day 12 — Grace in the Gray Areas

I choose grace where differences live.

Different is not wrong—it's refining.

Peace will lead me in every gray space.

Differences don't divide us when grace defines us.

Day 13 — Seeing Him as God Sees Him

I will see my husband through God's eyes.

I will cover with prayer, not critique.

Grace will shape my vision and my voice.

When I look through heaven's lens, love always comes into focus.

Day 14 — Bite Your Tongue, Bless Instead

I will bless instead of bite.

The Holy Spirit will guard my mouth.

My words will plant peace and pull up offense.

Every withheld word can become a seed of blessing instead.

Day 15 — Let Love Lead

Love will go first in me.

Peace, not pride, will set my tone.

Where love leads, offense loses.

Love leads the way when pride steps aside.

Day 16 — The Beauty of Silence

I will choose peaceful silence over prideful noise.

My stillness will make space for God to speak.

His peace will fight battles my words never could.

In the quiet, God says more than I ever could with my words.

Day 17 — Forgiveness in Real Time

I will forgive quickly and completely.

Offense will not take root in my heart.

Grace will flow through me the moment I'm hurt.

Forgiveness frees me faster than time ever could.

Day 18 — Choosing Gratitude Mid-Conflict

I will give thanks in every circumstance.

Gratitude will disarm offense and shift my focus.

Peace will guard my heart even in conflict.

Gratitude turns conflict into connection and tension into tenderness.

Day 19 — Rewriting the Narrative

I will take every thought captive to truth.

My mind will agree with God, not assumption.

Grace will rewrite the stories offense once told.

The truth I choose to believe becomes the peace I get to live.

Day 20 — Protecting His Reputation

I will honor my husband with my words.

Loyalty will lead my conversations.

My speech will protect, not expose, the man I love.

Honor is the quiet language of love that builds lasting trust.

Day 21 — When He Doesn't Notice You

God sees me fully, even when others don't.

My worth is anchored in His gaze, not human attention.

I am seen, known, and cherished by the One who never overlooks me.

When I rest in being seen by God, I stop striving to be noticed by man.

Day 22 — The Ministry of Listening

I will listen to understand, not to reply.

My silence will create safety, my attention will build trust.

Every moment I truly hear becomes holy ground.

Listening is one of the holiest ways to love.

Day 23 — Humility Heals

I choose humility over pride and healing over being right.

My softness invites God's strength.

Grace will speak louder than my need to win.

Humility opens the door where pride once built walls.

Day 24 — Guarding Your Heart Without Hardening It

I will guard my heart with grace, not walls.

Love will flow freely through the gates of discernment.

My softness is my strength, and peace is my protection.

A guarded heart stays soft when grace holds the gate.

Day 25 — Peace Over Proving Your Point

I will choose peace over pride and connection over control.

My calm will carry more power than any argument.

Where peace leads, God's presence abides.

Peace wins battles pride can't even enter.

Day 26 — Speak Life

I will plant life with my tongue.

My words will build, not break.

Encouragement will be the atmosphere of my home.

When I speak life, I sound like love.

Day 27 — Rest from Resentment

I lay down resentment and receive rest.

I release what I cannot carry to Jesus.

My heart will breathe in grace and exhale peace.

Rest begins where resentment ends.

Day 28 — Love Without a Hook

I will love with no strings attached.

Obedience, not outcome, will steady my heart.

I will sow grace and let God bring the harvest.

Unconditional love frees both the giver and the receiver.

Day 29 — Grace on Repeat

I will press reset with grace again.

His mercies renew me daily; mine will too.

Progress, not perfection, will mark my love.

Grace on repeat is how transformation takes root.

Day 30 — Unoffendable Love

I put on unoffendable love.

Peace will rule my responses.

Rooted in grace, I will not be shaken.

This is the fruit of every surrender — love that can't be shaken.

About THE AUTHOR

Hey friend, I'm **Misty**.

I'm a wife, a mama of nine, and a woman who's seen firsthand how God can redeem what once felt beyond repair. My story is one of running, breaking, and being found by a love that never gave up on me.

For years, I tried to fix everything on my own...my marriage, my emotions, my past, but it wasn't until I finally surrendered that I discovered what true freedom felt like. My first book, *He Was Always There*, tells the story of that redemption, the long road from rebellion and addiction to restoration and grace.

This book, *The Unoffendable Wife*, is the next chapter of that story. It was born in the quiet, ordinary moments of marriage, the eye rolls, misunderstandings, and daily choices that reveal what's really in our hearts.

Through it, God taught me that peace doesn't come from perfect circumstances; it comes from a softened heart that trusts Him more than pride.

Today, my greatest joy is helping other women experience that same transformation, to find healing, hope, and holy peace right where they are. Whether through writing, coaching, or sharing online, my heartbeat is to remind you that it's never too late to start again, love deeper, and live unoffendably.

When I'm not writing, you'll probably find me at home in Florida with my husband, Matt, surrounded by our big, beautiful, loud family...cooking, laughing, or planning our next adventure.

Let's stay connected: mistyparenzan.com

@mistyparenzan   Misty Parenzan